OECD Reviews of Vocational Education and Training

Apprenticeship in England, United Kingdom

Małgorzata Kuczera, Simon Field

OECD
BETTER POLICIES FOR BETTER LIVES

Please cite this publication as:
Kuczera, M. and S. Field (2018), *Apprenticeship in England, United Kingdom*, OECD Reviews of Vocational Education and Training, OECD Publishing, Paris
http://dx.doi.org/10.1787/9789264298507-en

ISBN 978-92-64-29847-7 (print)
ISBN 978-92-64-29850-7 (PDF)

Series: OECD Reviews of Vocational Education and Training
ISSN 2077-7728 (print)
ISSN 2077-7736 (online)

Photo credits: Cover © LituFalco - Fotolia.com.

Corrigenda to OECD publications may be found on line at: *www.oecd.org/about/publishing/corrigenda.htm*.

Foreword

Like many countries, England has identified in apprenticeship a model of vocational learning which has not only stood the test of time, but is also relevant to the requirements of modern economies. England has committed itself to a very ambitious programme to develop apprenticeship, with a new funding arrangement in the form of an employer levy, and major reforms of the apprenticeship system including the development of new apprenticeship standards created in close consultation with employers, and an overall aim of increasing both the quality and quantity of apprenticeships. The energy which England is currently investing in these reforms is impressive and encouraging. But many challenges remain in implementing current reforms effectively, and realising the goal of a world class apprenticeship system.

This OECD report, *Apprenticeship in England, United Kingdom*, supports the reform efforts, by comparing the reforms in England with the experience and example of other countries. Among many recommendations, the report argues for more general education in all apprenticeships for young people; an increased emphasis on supporting work-based learning; and clear logical relationships between apprenticeship and the technical qualifications now under development. Degree apprenticeships potentially represent an important opportunity, but they need to involve a real integration of study in a university with work-based learning, not just a part-time degree plus a job.

This report was drafted by Małgorzata Kuczera and Simon Field. Elisa Larrakoetxea and Jennifer Cannon provided valuable administrative support. The OECD is very grateful to colleagues in England, in the Department for Education (DfE) and many other people we met during our visits for their many very constructive contributions to the review, in particular James Davison, Simon McKee and Frank Bowley from the DfE, Alex Wilson and Mike Keogh from the Institute for Apprenticeship. Within the OECD the report benefited from many helpful comments and advice from Anthony Mann.

Table of contents

Tables

Figures

Boxes

Executive summary

Across many countries, apprenticeship is now experiencing a revival, in the light of a wide range of evidence demonstrating its effectiveness as a means of transitioning young people into work, and serving the economy. But few countries can match the energy and range of reforms currently being pursued in England.

Key findings

England has launched a series of reforms that champion the historically neglected institution of apprenticeship, and address some previous weaknesses, by encouraging more substantive apprenticeship programmes and a stronger funding framework. Alongside wider reforms in the qualifications system, they replace a proliferation of competing and overlapping qualifications with apprenticeship standards developed with employers for each occupation. They are backed by high-quality analysis, and increasingly rich data sources. Collectively this involves a concerted and serious attempt to develop a high-quality apprenticeship system in England. Despite these strengths, there is still some way to go to establish an apprenticeship system in England to match those of the strongest countries. International comparison suggests several ways in which reforms might be adapted to achieve higher quality and better outcomes.

Key messages

Promoting and strengthening youth apprenticeship

While England faces major challenges in transitioning young people from school to work, youth apprenticeship currently makes a limited contribution to this task, as most recent growth has been in adult apprentices. The government should seek an expansion of quality youth apprenticeships, as in other countries, where such apprenticeships play a major role. Youth apprenticeships should provide more general education, including for apprentices that already have Level 2 English and maths qualifications. This would help all apprentices to develop the study skills necessary for further learning and successful careers. The eligibility of apprentices aged 16-19 for social benefits should also be re-appraised, recognising that the attractiveness of apprenticeship needs to be sustained.

Engaging employers in work-based learning

In England, the historic responsibility of employers to deliver work-based learning to apprentices has been largely eclipsed by a focus on training delivered by a third-party training provider. This is unfortunate, as the key advantage of apprenticeship over other forms of vocational training is work-based learning, delivered by experienced workplace practitioners. Employer engagement should be encouraged by introducing clear standards for work-based learning, and investing in the training capacity of employers. Regulations and standards should also ensure that apprentices are not used solely as unskilled labour, recognising that in England nearly one in five apprentices is paid below the legal minimum.

Ensuring funding through the levy

While the introduction of the apprenticeship levy may encourage larger levy-paying employers to meet more of their skills needs through apprenticeships, meeting levy requirements in this way may not always make the best contribution to skills development. The strongest possible quality assurance measures will be needed to ensure that the replacement of other training by fundable apprenticeships genuinely adds value. An effective apprenticeship system involves various elements such as the development of the apprentice in the workplace by the employer and the broader education of young apprentices. While it may not be appropriate to fund all these activities through the levy, they do need to be supported, funded where necessary and their quality assured.

Quality in apprentice qualifications and assessment

While some strong principles are now in place, implementing an effective apprentice qualification system poses significant challenge. First, apprentice qualifications need to be clearly articulated with associated T-levels, so that apprentices can see what programmes of study are needed to enter target careers. Second, apprenticeship qualifications need to be sufficiently broad, and therefore few in number. This means keeping the total number of apprenticeship standards well under one thousand, in common with the approach of other countries. Third, it means developing clear arrangements to allow informally acquired skills to be certified through the end-point assessments associated with apprenticeships. Fourth, it means reviewing current plans for competition in the assessment market, as such competition will make it very difficult to realise consistency in assessment standards.

Equity and social mobility

New apprenticeship standards are, rightly, intended to be more demanding, but low-skilled school leavers will need preparation and support if they are to succeed in this more demanding environment, recognising that dropout is already a challenge, and by international standards, teenagers in England have relatively weak basic skills. Traineeships are promising, but are still relatively small-scale. The reformed apprenticeship system will need to include and engage those from disadvantaged backgrounds, and those who leave school with few skills. Building on the experience of traineeships, England should further explore, in the light of evidence and experience, pre-apprenticeship and alternative apprenticeship programmes that effectively prepare young people to undertake a full apprenticeship, equip them with basic and employability skills, and grant them workplace experience and career advice.

Special types of apprenticeship

Different economic sectors and different types of apprenticeship present special challenges. Degree apprenticeships are likely to grow rapidly as they allow those involved to avoid student loans and subsequent debt. This will be a positive development, but only if it restructures university degrees into quality apprenticeships with a substantial element of work-based learning, rather than just a part-time degree plus a job. Small employers play a big role in apprenticeship provision, and may need special support, including advice on how to make most effective use of apprenticeship, and local networks of co-operation. The rationale for the new apprentice target for public-sector employers is questionable, given that the public-sector workforce is already relatively skilled in comparison with the private sector.

Chapter 1. Assessment and recommendations

This first chapter describes the main characteristics of English apprenticeship in comparison with those of other countries. In England, apprenticeships are much shorter than in many countries and many current apprentices are incumbent workers. England is also distinctive in the lack of emphasis on employer-provided training. This chapter describes the current reforms aiming to expand and improve the quality of apprenticeship. It then sets out an assessment of the direction of reform and the challenges that remain, and summarises the suggestions for policy advanced in depth in later chapters of the report.

Introduction: Why apprenticeship matters

Apprenticeship is now experiencing a global revival

After a period of relative neglect in many countries, apprenticeship is now experiencing a revival, in the light of a wide range of evidence demonstrating its effectiveness as a means of transitioning young people into work, and serving the economy. The prevalence of apprenticeship is highly variable (see Figure 1.1). Few countries can match the energy and range of reforms currently being pursued in England, including an ongoing reform of the content of apprenticeship programmes and how they are assessed, a complete restructuring of funding through the introduction of the apprenticeship levy, a target of three million apprenticeship starts by 2020, and new targets for apprenticeships in the public sector. These reforms are designed to address multiple policy challenges, such as the need to encourage employers to invest more in skills, concern to develop more effective education and training pathways for young people who do not go to university, and a move to correct some serious quality weaknesses in apprenticeships as previously delivered.

Figure 1.1. There are large differences in the use of apprenticeship across countries

Current apprentices in programmes leading to upper secondary or shorter post-secondary qualifications as a share of all students enrolled in upper secondary and shorter post-secondary education (ISCED 3 and ISCED 4C), 16-65 year-olds (2012)

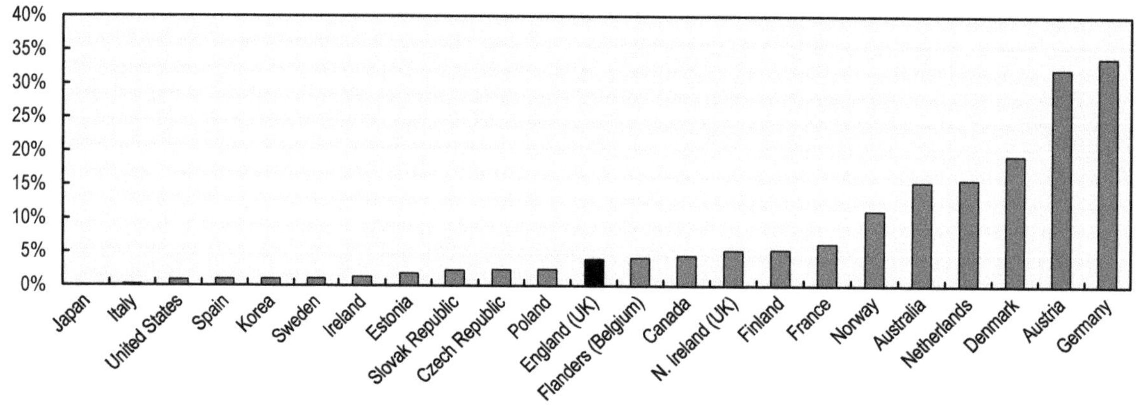

Note: In England, there are no qualifications classified at ICED 4C level. The data are based on self-report and may therefore undercount apprentices in England given evidence that some of them are not aware that they are apprentices. In Japan, Italy, the United States, Spain, Sweden, Korea and Ireland the estimated share of current apprentices is not significantly different from zero. ISCED: International Standard Classification of Education, www.uis.unesco.org/Education/Documents/isced-2011-en.pdf.

Source: OECD (2016), *Survey of Adult Skills (PIAAC)* (Database 2012, 2015), www.oecd.org/skills/piaac/publicdataandanalysis/.

StatLink http://dx.doi.org/10.1787/888933698944

This OECD study takes place in the context of these reforms

While there have been several recent reviews of apprenticeship policy in England, the aim of this report is to compare the English apprenticeship system with those of other leading apprenticeship countries, and make policy suggestions on that basis. The work involved study missions to England by the OECD team, and discussions with a wide variety of stakeholders, but also draws extensively on the OECD's range of data, knowledge and experience of the apprenticeship systems of other countries as well as in England.

Subsequent chapters of this report look at different aspects of apprenticeship

This first chapter aims to set the scene. It describes the main characteristics of English apprenticeship in comparison with those of other countries, and describes the current reforms in England. It then sets out an assessment of the direction of reform, and the challenges that remain, and summarises the suggestions for policy advanced in depth in later chapters of the report. Subsequent chapters examine different topics by introducing the challenge (*Challenge*), advancing policy suggestions (*Policy pointer*), providing arguments for the proposed policy solutions and discussing how these policy solutions could be implemented in the English context (*Analysis*). Chapter 2 assesses whether sufficient general education is included within youth apprenticeships and some potential incentives for individuals and employers to engage in youth apprenticeships. Chapter 3 looks at work-based learning, an issue which is not salient in policy discussion in England, and at a connected risk that apprenticeship might be used as a source of cheap unskilled labour. Chapter 4 compares the apprenticeship levy with levies in other countries, and explores potential incentive effects. Chapter 5 addresses quality in the apprenticeship qualifications system, in terms of the number of apprenticeship qualifications and their articulation with other vocational qualifications, and the role of the market in assessments. Chapter 6 looks at equity, exploring how disadvantaged and under-performing students may be prepared for apprenticeship, and helped to succeed within apprenticeship programmes. Chapter 7 explores policy issues related to different types of apprenticeships in different sectors, including degree apprenticeships, targets in the public sector, and apprenticeships for smaller employers.

The characteristics of English apprenticeship

Apprenticeship numbers have increased dramatically in the last two decades

In England, about half a million apprenticeship starts take place every year, with men and women roughly equally represented. These figures represent dramatic increases from the late 1990s, when the equivalent figure was less than 100 000. Most of the growth has been in older apprentices, with starts for those over 25 more than quadrupling from just under 50 000 in 2009/10 to more than 200 000 in 2015/16. Starts for those under 19 have only increased by about 10% over the same period, to reach 131 000 in 2015/16. Starts for higher-level apprenticeships have increased faster than for Level 2 apprenticeships, but Level 2 apprenticeships still represented nearly 60% of the total in 2015/16 (House of Commons, 2016).

In England, unlike some other countries, relatively few apprentices are in the skilled trades and crafts

The popular image of an apprentice is often someone working in a skilled trade, and this accurately reflects some apprenticeship systems, for example in Ireland (Kis, 2010). But in England nearly three-quarters of apprentice starts in 2015/16 were in three sectors: business administration and law; health, public service and care; and retail and commercial (House of Commons, 2016). This is a recent phenomenon – in the mid-1990s, most of the apprenticeships were in more traditional trade fields such as construction and engineering (Lanning, 2011). Since then, growth in service sector apprenticeships, many of them for older incumbent workers, and often involving some recognition of prior learning and more limited amounts of actual training, have radically changed the picture. Some similar trends have been apparent in Australia (see Box 1.1). An important minority of apprenticeships continue to take a more traditional form. In the engineering and construction sectors apprenticeships often last three years, and are mostly for young people recruited as school leavers as a means of providing skills for the future.

Box 1.1. The changing face of Australian apprenticeships

Apprenticeships and traineeships play a major role in the Australian skills system, with around one-quarter of a million enrolments – although numbers have been falling in the last five years. 'Traineeships' are a form of apprenticeship, with a similar mix of work-based learning and off-the-job classroom programmes. Apprenticeships are identified in 'trade' areas, such as engineering, automotive, carpentry and the like and are typically three or four years of training, and traineeships in 'non-trade' areas, including community and personal service, retail and clerical roles, typically at lower qualification levels and involving often only one or two years of training. Since their introduction in the 1980s, the non-trade traineeships have grown rapidly. Thus, the non-trade sector grew from around one-quarter of the total enrolment (in apprenticeships and traineeships) in the mid-1990s to become the larger part of the enrolled population by 2012, although numbers in the non-trade areas have since fallen sharply. Both apprenticeships and traineeships are referred to below under the title of 'apprenticeships'.

This sectoral shift has been linked to sharp growth in the proportion of adult apprentices (aged 25 and above). While in 1996 adult apprentices were a small minority, only representing 8% of trade apprenticeships (at a time when most apprenticeships were in the trades) by 2016 adult apprentices were nearly one-third of trade apprenticeships and nearly one-half of non-trade apprenticeships. These adult apprentices are much more likely to be incumbent workers rather than new recruits. Adult apprentices are also more likely to take advantage of opportunities to use the recognition of prior learning to realise an accelerated completion of their apprenticeships – so that around half of the adult apprentices reduced their apprenticeship period from 3-4 years to less than 2 years.

Source: NCVER (2017a), *Data Slicer: Apprentices and Trainees December 2016*, www.ncver.edu.au/data/data/all-data/data-slicer-apprentices-and-trainees-december-2016; NCVER (2017b), *Historical Time Series of Apprenticeships and Traineeships in Australia from 1963 to 2017*, www.ncver.edu.au/data/data/all-data/historical-time-series-tables; Hargreaves, J., J. Stanwick and P. Skujins (2017), *The Changing Nature of Apprenticeships: 1996–2016,* National Centre for Vocational Education Research, Adelaide, Australia; Knight, B. and T. Karmel (2011), *Apprenticeships and Traineeships in Australia*, Institute for Public Policy Research, London, United Kingdom, www.ippr.org/files/images/media/files/publication/2011/10/rethinking-apprenticeships_3-2_Oct2011_8028.pdf.

English apprenticeships are much shorter than in many countries

As indicated in Table 1.1, despite a recent requirement that all apprenticeships should be at least one year in length, English apprenticeships are typically much shorter than in many other countries, with an average of less than 18 months, compared with 3-4 years in some other countries (Department for Education, 2016). English apprentices therefore commonly spend less time in total in education and training than those in many other countries. A 3- or 4-year apprenticeship in Denmark, Norway, Austria, Switzerland or Germany will involve a substantial amount of general education, provided off the job – this may be of the order of 400 hours – a point discussed more fully in Chapter 3. This contrasts with the English and maths requirements in an English apprenticeship, which are primarily remedial, and if they apply will involve only around 50 hours of study. Youth apprentices in England therefore receive much less academic preparation than those in the other countries mentioned.

Table 1.1. The duration of apprenticeship programmes and how apprentices spend their time

	Duration of the programme including off-the-job period and work placement with the company	Time allocation in apprenticeship programmes	Workplace time spent in productive and non–productive tasks
Austria	3-4 years	66% - work place 20% - off-the-job education and training 14% - leave and sick days	83% of the time with the company is spent on productive work
Denmark	3.5-4 years (typically)	Missing	Missing
England	Min 12 months -average around 18 months	At least 20% in off-the-job education and training, (sometimes in the workplace but outside productive work).	
Germany	2-3.5 years	56% - work place 29% - off-the-job education and training 14% - leave and sick days	77% of the time with the company is spent on productive work
Netherlands	2-4 years		
Norway	Mostly 4 years (Shorter programmes are available for disadvantaged students)	(typically, first two years are spent in school and the last two with the company)	1 year of training 1 year of productive work
Sweden	3 years	Apprentices spend as much time in school as in a work place with the company	Missing
Switzerland	3-4 years (2-year programmes are available for disadvantaged students)	59% - work place 27% - off-the-job education and training 14% - leave and sick days	83% of the time with the company is spent on productive work

Source: Kuczera M. (2017), "Striking the right balance: Costs and benefits of apprenticeship", *OECD Education Working Papers*, No. 153, http://dx.doi.org/10.1787/995fff01-en.

In England, around half of starting apprentices are incumbent workers

In England around half of apprentices are incumbent workers, a proportion that has been growing over time, with the other half recruited to be apprentices – not all of them starting their training immediately (DfE, 2016). This means that the function of apprenticeship in England is equally divided between skills development for the workforce and initial recruitment. This is closely tied to the age of the apprentices – with nearly 90% of those aged under 19 recruited as apprentices, but only just over 10% of those aged 25 and over. Service sector apprentices are much more likely to be incumbent workers – with more than 60% of starting apprentices being so in retail and health sectors. Conversely in the construction sector, the overwhelming majority – nearly 85% of starting apprentices – are recruited as apprentices (DfE, 2016).

This contrasts with some, but not all other apprenticeship systems

Different countries have very different age mixes in their apprenticeship systems. In Norway, for example, apprenticeship is primarily about transition from school to work and the apprentice population is dominated by young people in upper secondary education. But England's position is not unique. In the United States and Canada, apprentices are typically in their late 20s (see Figure 1.2), while in Australia, older incumbent workers have become more common among apprenticeship and traineeship starters (see Box 1.1). In Germany in 2014 around 56% of apprentices were under 20, and a further 20% were between 21 and 23 years old, the older apprentices being a mix of those who complete the academic upper secondary *Abitur* before entering apprenticeship, and others who have often passed through pre-apprenticeship programmes. Conversely in Switzerland the vast majority of apprentices are young – three-quarters were under 20 in 2014/15 (Muehlemann, 2016). Apprentices in England have an ordinary employment contract, rather than the special apprenticeship contract which is found in most apprenticeships in continental Europe, as for example in Germany and Norway. In this respect England is similar to several other countries where apprentices are seen as regular employees (see ILO-World Bank, 2013).

Figure 1.2. Share of 25-year-olds and older among current apprentices (2012, 2014)

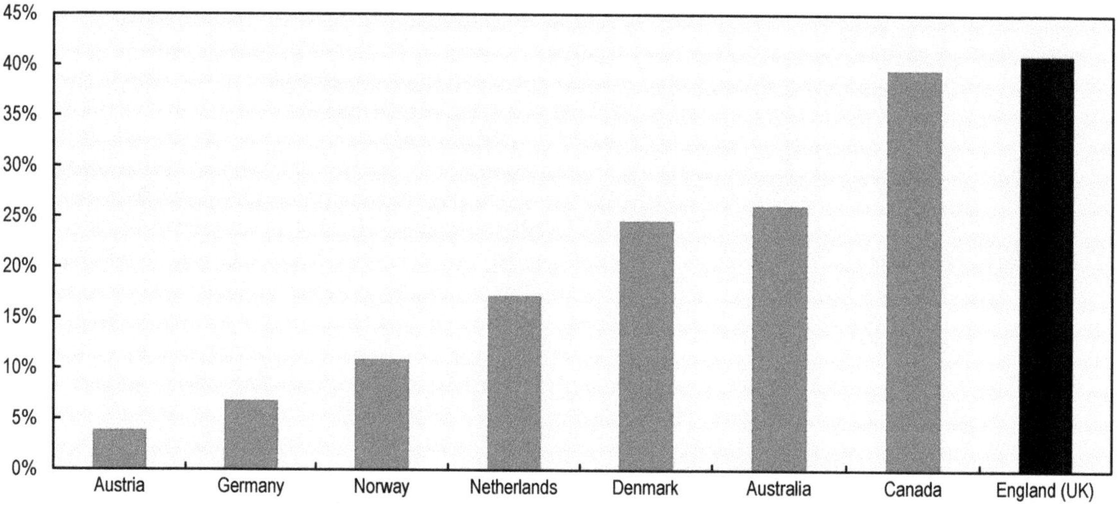

Source: Kuczera, M. (2017), "Striking the right balance: Costs and benefits of apprenticeship", *OECD Education Working Papers*, No. 153, http://dx.doi.org/10.1787/995fff01-en; Data for England: BIS (2014), "Apprenticeships Evaluation: Learner Survey", *BIS Research Paper*, No. 205, www.gov.uk/government/publications/apprenticeships-evaluation-learner-survey-2014.

StatLink http://dx.doi.org/10.1787/888933698963

The funding and governance is also distinctive

In many apprenticeship systems, little money changes hands other than apprentice wages. Resourcing instead depends on in-kind provision, according to the defined responsibilities of the different parties in the apprenticeship. So, in most apprenticeships in continental Europe, the apprentice works and studies, the employer trains the apprentice on the job, and the vocational school provides the off-the-job training and education. (Adult apprentices sometimes pay tuition fees.) Sometimes apprenticeship systems are supported by government subsidies for participant employers (see Chapter 4). Quality assurance is not linked to financial flows, but to the relative responsibilities of the different parties, so the training provided by the employer is quality assured even though it is not publicly funded.

In England, financial flows drive the apprenticeship system

In England flows of money in different markets drive much of the system. This is because the main regulated element of apprenticeship is off-the-job training, and this training is offered by multiple competing training providers, funded according to various rules, primarily from public money. Historically, awarding bodies competed to market the mini-qualifications that make up apprenticeship frameworks, and these were paid for by the training providers that competed to deliver apprenticeships, drawing down government funding when they did so. While the levy represents a significant reform, flows of money and the incentives they create will continue to drive the system. Quality assurance will continue to follow the flows of money, through approvals of training providers and assessment bodies according to set criteria, and in Ofsted inspections of funded bodies and their activities for which they receive funds. The extensive policy debates in England, which emerge from the driving force of funding, about funding rules and the incentives they create, therefore have limited resonances in continental Europe, but do find more parallels, for example, in Australia, where many private training providers compete to provide the classroom training of apprentices. See Box 1.2 for the definition of the off-the-job training in England.

Box 1.2. Off-the-job training in England

In England, off-the-job training is defined in the apprenticeship funding rules as learning which is undertaken outside of the normal day-to-day working environment and leads towards the achievement of an apprenticeship. This can include training that is delivered at the apprentice's normal place of work but must not be delivered as part of their normal working duties.

The off-the-job training must be directly relevant to the apprenticeship framework or standard and could include the following:

- The teaching of theory (for example: lectures, role playing, simulation exercises, online learning or manufacturer training).
- Practical training: shadowing, mentoring, industry visits and attendance at competitions.
- Learning support and time spent writing assessments/assignments.

Off-the-job training does not include:

- English and maths (up to Level 2) which is funded separately.
- Progress reviews or on-programme assessment needed for an apprenticeship framework or standard.
- Training which takes place outside the apprentice's paid working hours.

Source: Education and Skills Funding Agency (2017), *Apprenticeship Funding and Performance-Management Rules For Training Providers*, www.gov.uk/government/uploads/system/uploads/attachment_data/file/646244/17_18_apprenticeships_funding_and_pm_rules_V4.pdf.

England is also distinctive in the lack of emphasis on employer-provided training

Linked to the way in which flows of money drive the system, the focus of policy is funding, and the training which is funded. This is the off-the-job training offered by a registered training provider (recognising that some of the off-the-job training can be provided in the workplace, according to the definition of off-the-job training in England). As discussed in Chapter 3, England is unusual, both relative to other countries, and relative to the historical tradition of apprenticeship, in imposing very few training obligations on employers that take apprentices. This leaves the traditional heart of apprenticeship – training provided in the workplace by an employer – in a marginal position, as it is not subject to regulatory standards. While employers commonly (although certainly not invariably) do train their apprentices, formally and informally, much of this takes place outside the regulated structure of the apprenticeship system.

Policy development: Current and recent reforms

The expansion and improvement of apprenticeship is a major policy target

During recent years, apprenticeship in England has been undergoing extensive reform. Four main pillars of reform can be identified – more substantive and better-quality apprenticeship following the Richard review with the requirement of 20% of the programme duration spent on off-the-job training; reform in the vocational qualification system following the Sainsbury review; growth in apprentice numbers through numerical targets; and funding reform through the introduction of the apprenticeship levy- and non-levy-paying employers funding 10% of the apprenticeship cost (with the exception of SMEs and apprenticeships provided to 16-18 year-olds).

The Richard review recommended both more substantive and better-quality programmes

Prior to the Richard review, apprenticeship programmes had sometimes been completed in weeks or months, and sometimes involved little or no training, with apprenticeship often being used to certify existing skills; nearly half of all apprenticeships occupied less than one year. All apprenticeship programmes now require at least one year, and 20% of working time must be devoted to training. Apprenticeship 'frameworks' which build up apprenticeships as an à la carte package of mini-qualifications are gradually being replaced by apprenticeship standards which are intended to be more demanding. Each apprenticeship 'standard' sets out the package of skills, knowledge and behaviours required for a target occupation, and that standard is accompanied by an 'assessment plan'. Standards and assessment plans are developed by groups of (at least 10) employers and are subject to approval by the newly established Institute for Apprenticeships (IfA). This process has many similarities to that adopted by other apprenticeship countries (see Box 1.3). The number of apprentices pursuing standards has been rising. In 2016/17 there were 23 700 starts on new standards as compared to 3 800 the year before (DfE, 2017b). Employers may choose training providers and end-point assessors from a set of bodies approved for these purposes.

A simplified principle of one apprenticeship standard for each occupation has been introduced

In the past, England maintained thousands of vocational qualifications, including those which were built up into apprentice qualifications in apprentice frameworks. Given recommendations in Richard (2012), the Sainsbury review and in a previous OECD review (Musset and Field, 2013), there will be a new approach, based on the principle that there should be one apprenticeship standard for each occupation. Although this represents a radical change in England, it brings England into line with most other major apprenticeship countries, and is very much to be welcomed. Funding bands for training providers vary by level and subject area with higher bands for apprenticeships with higher-cost training, including apprenticeships in STEM. The new Institute for Apprenticeship will have oversight not only of the apprenticeship standards but also the new vocational qualifications, with an emphasis on the quality and coherence of the vocational system, subdivided into 15 pathways.

Numerical targets have been set

An overall target of 3 million apprenticeship starts by 2020 has been set, backed by a new expectation that a minimum of 2.3% of the workforce of larger (250+ employees) public-sector employers should be apprentices (BIS, 2016a) – it is noted that there are no targets for individual employers. The aim is to treble the number of apprenticeships in food, farming and agri-tech, increase the proportion of apprenticeship uptake by black and minority ethnic communities by 20% by 2020, and roll out many more degree apprenticeships (BIS, 2016b).

An apprenticeship levy has been introduced

From 2017, employers will pay 0.5% of their payroll over GBP 3M (thus excluding small employers). Levy funds will be made available to levy-paying and non-levy-paying employers to fund apprenticeship training and the associated end-point assessments (see SFA, 2017). When the apprenticeship levy was announced it was framed in terms of training away from the workplace (e.g. Budget statement, 2015: "This approach will reverse the long-term trend of employer underinvestment in training, which has seen the number of employees who attend a training course away from the workplace fall from 141 000 in 1995 to 18 000 in 2014", HM Treasury, 2015, pp.60). However, the levy has been implemented more broadly and it can be used to fund any training by an apprentice as long as that apprentice is not working (off-the-job training). The levy is discussed in detail in Chapter 4.

Box 1.3. How vocational education training (VET) programmes are created in Switzerland and Norway

In **Switzerland** VET programmes are developed by the private sector, i.e. employers and professional organisations. When a professional organisation wishes to introduce a VET programme for a new occupation, it works closely with the other main partners (i.e. the Confederation - federal government, and the cantons). The occupational field and the labour market demand in that occupation need to be confirmed.

The VET programme is launched based on the job profile, the overview of all professional competences and the level of difficulty of the given occupation. The federal State Secretariat for Education, Research and Innovation (SERI) examines the proposed draft 'ordinance' (legally establishing the programme) and training plan for quality control purposes. Following any necessary adjustments, SERI organises a consultation session with cantonal agencies, federal agencies and other interested parties which may lead to further adjustments in the VET ordinance and training plan before it is approved and launched. The committee responsible for the given occupation will then meet at least every five years to re-examine the VET programme and update it in the light of developments in the industry sector.

Norway has just reformed the process of defining the content of apprenticeship programmes drawing on the positive results of a two-year pilot study.

The reform has reinforced the role of professional councils involving employers and employees representatives (social partners). In the past social partners advised on the content of training provided in the third year of apprenticeship programmes by employers. Now they have a decisive role on the training provided by employers. The government has to take into account social partners' propositions unless the propositions are against the law or involve an important increase in public spending. Social partners maintain their advisory role regarding the content of the first two years of apprenticeships that are provided in school.

Source: Adapted from (SERI) (2016), *Vocational and Professional Education and Training in Switzerland, Facts and Figures* 2016, www.eda.admin.ch/content/dam/countries/countries-content/canada/en/Vocational-and-professional-education-and-training-switzerland_E.pdf; Utdanningsdirektoratet (2017), Retningslinjer for samarbeid – SRY, faglige råd og Udir, https://fagligerad.files.wordpress.com/2016/05/retningslinjer-samarbeid-for-sry-fagligerad-udir.pdf.

The policy debate

A sequence of policy reports over 2016 and 2017 have examined current reforms

A first study by the Institute for Public Policy Research (IPPR) (Pullen and Clifton, 2016) pointed to the reliance of the economy on low skills as a factor that would not simply be overcome through stronger apprenticeships. Pullen and Dromey (2016) looked at the challenges faced by 16-18 year-olds, and argued that lower level (Level 2) apprenticeships for this age group are weak, since they are too job-specific, often only one year long and do not include sufficient general education. They argue for their replacement by a distinct pre-apprenticeship programme, to include more general education, such as English and maths, with one pre-apprenticeship programme for each of the 15 Sainsbury pathways. In a study for the Institute of Fiscal Studies, Amin-Smith et al., (2017) argue that there is a risk that the target of three million apprentices may be at the expense of quality, and are particularly critical of the public-sector target which they see as arbitrary. A parliamentary select committee report (House of Commons, 2017) argues for more emphasis on outcome measures alongside the target of three million starts and that levy funding should prioritise industry sectors and parts of the country where skills development is most needed. All the reports express concern that the levy may lead to mere rebadging of existing training arrangements to become fundable under the levy. Both Amin-Smith et al., (2017) and the select committee also express concern about a one-size-fits-all approach to the public sector. In a new report on skills in England the OECD (2017) argue, in respect of apprenticeship, that more rigorous standards are needed for the type and quality of on-the-job training, and that more emphasis should be given to helping employers see the business case for apprenticeship.

Assessment: Strengths

Current reforms represent a serious attempt to develop a high-quality apprenticeship system

The apprenticeship reforms in England have many strengths. They champion the historically neglected institution of apprenticeship, address head-on some of its previous weaknesses by requiring or encouraging more substantive, demanding and higher-level programmes and provide an enabling funding framework. Alongside wider reforms in the qualifications system, they replace a dysfunctional proliferation of competing and overlapping qualifications, with a single apprenticeship standard developed with employers for each occupation. They are backed by high-quality analysis, and increasingly rich data sources. Collectively this involves a concerted and serious attempt to develop a high-quality apprenticeship system in England. More specifically:

Apprenticeship is being championed

Policy in England displays an unequivocal commitment to supporting apprenticeship, through reform of the content of apprenticeships following the Richard review, and of the funding system through the levy. Together, these place apprenticeship in a deservedly central place in the education and training system, recognising its proven strengths as a model of vocational learning.

Apprenticeships are more substantive and organised according to new standards

Recent reforms, following the 2012 Richard review, have made a good start in recovering from a position in which most apprenticeships were low level and insubstantive.

Apprenticeships now have a minimum length of one year, although average lengths are still half or less of those of other leading apprenticeship countries. The new standards are developed by employers and are consistent with the approach of many other strong apprenticeship countries.

A more transparent apprenticeship qualifications system is in place

Vocational qualifications, including apprenticeship programmes as frameworks, had become exceptionally diverse and fragmented, with large numbers of qualifications of limited labour market value. Following recommendations of the Richard, Sainsbury and OECD reviews, a strong principle is in place, in line with international best practice, in which there will be one apprentice standard per occupation. The remaining challenge, complementing this principle, is that of developing a clear logical relationship between apprenticeship and other vocational qualifications. This relationship should be addressed more readily through the joint responsibility for new T-levels and apprentice standards under the same regulatory roof in the Institute for Apprenticeships.

The levy may encourage apprenticeship

If levy-paying employers use rather than lose the funds that have accumulated in their digital levy accounts, they would seek ways of increasing the number or level of their apprenticeships. This may involve a substitution of apprenticeships for other ways of acquiring and developing workforce skills. The substitution of existing training by apprenticeships will be positive if robust quality assurance ensures that those apprenticeships are of high quality.

Traineeships are promising

The new traineeships appear to have positive outcomes. Although they are still small in scale relative the large pre-apprenticeship systems of some other countries, they provide a strong foundation for growth and development.

Data and evaluation are strong

As the reforms go forward, England will be powerfully assisted by increasingly good data on the outcomes of apprenticeship, and very good quality analysis of policy from diverse points of view.

But significant challenges remain

Despite these strengths, international comparison suggests that there is still a long way to go to establish an apprenticeship system in England to match those of the strongest countries. A large proportion of apprenticeships in England still involve low-level skills, acquired in a period of little more than a year, with a limited component of general education, and with most of the training taking place off the job. Work-based learning is under-developed. One in five apprentices is paid below the legal minimum wage, and there is limited support for those at risk of dropping out. In all these areas, improvements are needed. Many challenges are also emerging in realising the full implementation of the principles implicit in current reforms. International comparison suggests a number of ways in which reforms might be adapted to achieve higher quality and better outcomes for the English apprenticeship system. These are set out below in summary, and explained in depth in the remaining chapters of this report.

Assessment: Challenges and policy pointers

Promoting and strengthening youth apprenticeships (Chapter 2)

While England faces major challenges in transitioning young people from school to work, youth apprenticeship currently makes a limited contribution to this task, as most recent growth has been in adult apprentices. Young people in England perform less well on basic skills than their peers in many other OECD countries. Young apprentices in England, because they are treated as employees rather than students, do not receive the social benefits available to young apprentices in some other European countries. Compared to other countries, apprenticeship for young people also includes a relatively limited component of general education, including not just literacy and numeracy but wider topics that contribute to citizenship as well as further study.

Policy pointer 2.1: Promoting youth apprenticeships

In the light of a significant challenge of transitioning young people with poor school attainment into good quality jobs, the government should seek an expansion of quality youth apprenticeships, as in other countries, where such apprenticeships play a major role. Options include:

- Evaluate the impact of the existing wage setting on provision of apprenticeship by employers in different sectors, and on the uptake of apprenticeships by individuals across different age groups.
- Explore whether the threshold effect induced by a sharp wage increases when an apprentice turns 19 or completes the first year of apprenticeship may prevent employers from providing longer apprenticeships.
- Ensure that where youth apprentice wages are low, they are balanced by extensive benefits to the young apprentice in terms of the quality of the learning opportunities with the employer to avoid exploitation of youth apprentices as unskilled labour (as also argued in Chapter 3).
- In recognition of their status as a learner (as well as a worker), apprentices aged 16-19 (and their families) should be eligible for social benefits sufficiently attractive to allow youth apprenticeship to compete fairly, and without any bias in connection with social background, with other educational programmes for 16-19 year-olds.
- In line with other targets for apprenticeship, set up a target for an expansion of youth apprenticeships.

Policy pointer 2.2: Giving attention to wider education in youth apprenticeship

The broader education of young apprentices, including numeracy, literacy and digital skills, is extremely important. While more young people have weak numeracy and literacy skills in England than in many other countries, young apprentices receive less general education than their apprentice counterparts in many other countries. New requirements for the study of maths and English among apprentices are to be welcomed, but they do not go far enough. They do not address the needs for higher-level literacy and numeracy skills, and wider education, so as to support higher-level apprenticeships and pathways to further study.

In the long run, all apprenticeships should provide more general education, including for apprentices that already have Level 2 English and maths qualifications. More demanding requirements may be necessary for youth apprenticeships, for example through a pre-apprenticeship programme linked to a technical qualification, with general education as a precursor to a full apprenticeship. This would be consistent with the government's broader strategy for post-16 education.

Developing work-based learning (Chapter 3)

Historically, the defining feature of apprenticeship has been a contractual relationship between an apprentice who works and an employer who trains in return. In England, the responsibility of the employer to deliver training on the job has been largely eclipsed by a focus on training delivered usually by a third-party training provider. This is unfortunate, as the key advantage of apprenticeship over other forms of training is on-the-job training, delivered by experienced workplace practitioners. Nearly one in five apprentices are paid below the legal minimum, and even if apprentices receive the apprentice minimum wage there is a risk that they may be exploited as unskilled labour.

Policy pointer 3.1: Developing training on the job

As an integrated combination of external education and training and work-based learning is the most effective way of preparing apprentices for working life, employers should be encouraged to take more responsibility for work-based learning.

This can be achieved by introducing regulations and standards for work-based learning, and by investing in the training capacity of employers.

This may involve:

- Clarifying and strengthening, within the apprenticeship standards, what is expected of employers (as opposed to what is expected of training providers) in terms of work-based development that goes beyond the funded off-the-job training element. Work-based training should not only be fundable in principle, but encouraged or mandated systematically in all apprenticeships.
- Developing training for employer based supervisors of apprentices as part of a broader process of upgrading and professionalising work-based learning.
- Enhancing collaboration between training providers and employers, with training providers not only providing guidance to students in the workplace, but also providing guidance to workplace supervisors of apprentices over how practices at work can assist learning, and how productive work, linked to structured feedback on performance, can blend work and learning.
- Ensuring that apprenticeship is not used to exploit apprentices as unskilled labour through active enforcement of standards on employers.
- Enforcing rigorously the existing minimum wage requirements for apprentices.

Funding and the levy (Chapter 4)

While the introduction of the apprenticeship levy may encourage larger levy-paying employers to restructure and expand their training and skills development around apprenticeships, there is a risk that this might sometimes involve substitutions that meet levy requirements, but make more limited contributions to skills development. Some key parts of effective apprenticeship systems, are not funded through the levy, but do need to be supported in one way or another.

Policy pointer 4.1: Giving priority to quality

The introduction of the levy may have incentive effects on levy-paying employers, who will seek to increase apprentice numbers to spend their levy pots. Often this will involve restructuring other training and replacing other means of recruiting skilled workers. To ensure that the levy incentives work constructively, the strongest possible quality assurance measures will be needed so that apprenticeship training is of high quality, so that the restructuring involved adds value.

Policy pointer 4.2: Funding for an effective apprenticeship system

Under current rules, the apprenticeship levy provides funding for apprentice training and assessments delivered by registered training providers and assessment bodies, but not to other bodies or for other purposes. Quality assurance in the system primarily follows the funding, and therefore looks at these activities and bodies. However, an effective apprenticeship system involves a wide range of broader functions, including the development of the apprentice in the workplace by the employer (in parallel to any off-the-job training), the broader education of young apprentices, preparation for apprenticeship through traineeship and other pre-apprenticeship schemes, support and advice for apprentices and training employers seeking to get the best out of the apprenticeship system. While it may not be appropriate to fund all these activities through the levy, they do need to be supported, funded where necessary and their quality assured.

Quality in apprentice qualifications and assessment (Chapter 5)

While some strong principles are now in place, implementing an effective apprentice qualification system poses significant challenges. Apprenticeship qualifications need to be sufficiently broad, and few in number, to allow apprentice graduates to change employers and develop their careers, and to sustain the resource demand of continued updating. They will also need to be clearly articulated with associated T-levels, so that apprentices can see how to manage their programmes of study to realise the competences required for their target careers. The proposed competitive market in the provision of end-point assessments is an obstacle to consistency in standards. There is, as yet, no clear arrangement to allow informally acquired skills to be certified through the end-point assessments associated with apprenticeships, without going through an apprenticeship programme.

Policy pointer 5.1: Delivering a coherent apprenticeship qualifications system

A credible and robust system of apprentice qualifications needs to be coherent with the wider system of vocational qualifications and manageable in number. International experience offers some guidance:

- Apprentice standards represent the requirements for the target occupation, and should therefore be closely articulated with any related technical qualification. One option would be to require all graduates of associated technical qualifications to take the apprenticeship exam to certify their occupational competence. A second option would be to establish a technical qualification as a preparatory programme for a linked apprenticeship.
- To ensure the transferability of skills, the IfA needs to ensure that each proposed standard represents a wide occupational field and therefore reject proposals that do not do so, aiming to keep the eventual total number of standards well under one thousand.

- In the context of upskilling adult learners, a more effective framework for recognising prior learning needs to be developed within the frame of apprenticeship standards and levy funding. This will need to support the top-up training and assessments for those who are able to pass the end-point assessment, but have not pursued regular apprenticeships.

Policy pointer 5.2: Ensuring reliable end-point assessments

Few, if any, other countries seek to achieve consistency in assessment standards through multiple bodies conducting the assessment, and consistency in standards will be impossible to achieve with current plans for multiple assessment bodies for individual standards. Given the key role of consistent assessment standards in the credibility and reputation of apprentice qualifications these plans should be reviewed.

Equity and inclusion (Chapter 6)

New apprenticeship standards are, rightly, intended to be more demanding than previous apprenticeship qualifications. But this shift of the apprenticeship offer upmarket raises a challenge over how the system will serve the many low-skilled school leavers, who will need careful preparation and support if they are to succeed in this more demanding environment. One major challenge lies in whether labour market demand will also move upmarket to absorb the better skilled apprentice graduates. Traineeships are promising, but still relatively modest in number. Dropout from apprenticeship is already a challenge, and other things being equal, dropout rates might rise with more demanding standards and end-point assessments.

Policy pointer 6.1: Developing pre-apprenticeships and special apprenticeship schemes

A key element in the success of a reformed apprenticeship system will be its capacity to include and engage those from disadvantaged backgrounds, and those who leave school with few skills. Building on the experience of traineeships, further explore, in the light of evidence and experience, pre-apprenticeship and alternative apprenticeship programmes that effectively prepare young people to undertake a full apprenticeship, equip them with basic and employability skills, and grant them workplace experience and career advice.

Policy pointer 6.2: Supporting apprentices to successful completion

Consider establishing an apprenticeship support service. Through that service, offer targeted support to assist through to completion apprentices in need, or at risk. Such measures may include additional training in basic skills, mentoring and coaching, and other work-based measures.

Special types of apprenticeship (Chapter 7)

Different economic sectors and different types of apprenticeship present special challenges. Degree apprenticeships are likely to grow rapidly as they allow those involved to escape student loans. This will only be a positive development if it restructures university degrees into quality apprenticeships, rather than just a part-time degree plus a job. Small employers play a big role in apprenticeship provision, and may need special support to sustain further growth in their role. There are questions over the rationale for expecting large public-sector employers to invest in workforce skills (as well as taking more youth apprentices), given that the public-sector workforce is already relatively skilled.

Policy pointer 7.1: Securing a constructive use of degree apprenticeships

The expansion of degree apprenticeships should be a means of ensuring that the benefits of integrated on and off-the-job training are realised in these programmes rather than a means of restructuring full-time degrees as part-time merely to attract levy funds. To this end, ensure that all degree apprenticeships involve a clear commitment from employers to provide a substantial element of on-the-job training, closely aligned with the programme of studies pursued in a university. This proposal draws on the expectations for on-the-job training discussed in Chapter 3, and policy pointer 3.1.

Policy pointer 7.2: Supporting small and medium-sized employers

Small employers already make extensive use of apprenticeship in England. To support further growth and enhance quality, facilitate support services for smaller employers, advising them on how to make most effective use of apprenticeship, and supporting local networks of co-operation between employers with apprentices.

Policy pointer 7.3: Underpinning the public-sector target with wider policy goals

The public-sector workforce has better skills, on average, than the private sector. Any targets for the public sector might therefore be limited to the use of apprenticeship as a recruitment tool, in particular for youth apprenticeship.

Timescales and priorities for policy development and reform

The pace of reform is demanding

All the stakeholders in the English apprenticeship system are grappling with extensive change and reform on a scale unmatched by the experience of other countries. While supporting the overall direction of reform, this report makes suggestions for additional elements which need to be addressed to support high-quality apprenticeships. Clearly, implementing these suggestions could place additional burdens on the policy-making apparatus at a time when it is already under great pressure.

Reforms need to be prioritised, but some are urgent

This point is recognised. Some of the suggestions in this report, for example for stronger support services for smaller employers (see Chapter 7), are not necessarily immediate priorities. But some others are urgent, simply because of the pace of change. Chapter 3 points out the serious problem of apprentices being paid, unlawfully, less than the minimum wage, and the risk that apprentices, even if paid the minimum wage, might be exploited to perform unskilled work. If these problems are not tackled urgently they will stigmatise the whole apprentice brand. Chapter 5 of this report expresses concern about a potential rapid proliferation of over-numerous apprenticeship standards. If such proliferation takes place then it will be extremely difficult to prune back established standards to a more appropriate form and number. Chapter 7 sees degree apprenticeships as an opportunity, but also points to the risk that they could involve a pointless reshuffling of existing degrees into part-time degrees juxtaposed with a job, merely to attract levy funding. Here again, prevention will be much easier than cure. So overall, some triage of policy suggestions in this report according to urgency (as well as importance) will be necessary. Overall, this may raise questions about the pace of change. There will be a need for careful evaluation and monitoring of the reforms as they develop, and England has the data and analytic capacity to do this well. It will also be necessary to learn lessons from this emerging evidence, and change course when necessary.

Quality in apprenticeship is more important that quantitative targets

In sum therefore, the goal of quality in apprenticeships is paramount, and this will require substantial investment on several fronts, as set out in this report. Many of the quality requirements cannot be postponed. This goal of quality must also be a very clear priority, relative to quantitative targets, including the high-profile target of three million apprenticeship starts.

References

Amin-Smith, N., J. Cribb and L. Sibieta (2017), *Reforms to Apprenticeship Funding in England Institute for Fiscal Studies,* Institute for Fiscal Studies, London, United Kingdom, www.ifs.org.uk/uploads/publications/budgets/gb2017/gb2017ch8.pdf.

BIS (Department of Business, Innovation and Skills) (2016a), *Consultation on Apprenticeship Targets for Public Sector bodies*, BIS, Sheffield, United Kingdom, www.gov.uk/government/uploads/system/uploads/attachment_data/file/494493/bis-16-24-apprenticeship-targets-for-public-sector-bodies.pdf.

BIS (2016b), *BIS Single Departmental Plan: 2015-2020*, BIS, Sheffield, United Kingdom, www.gov.uk/government/publications/bis-single-departmental-plan-2015-to-2020/bis-single-departmental-plan-2015-to-2020.

BIS (2014), "Apprenticeships evaluation: Learner survey", *BIS Research Paper*, No. 205, BIS, London, United Kingdom, www.gov.uk/government/publications/apprenticeships-evaluation-learner-survey-2014.

DfE (Department for Education) (2017), *Apprenticeship Funding: How it Works*, www.gov.uk/government/publications/apprenticeship-levy-how-it-will-work/apprenticeship-levy-how-it-will-work.

DfE (2017), *Further Education and Skills in England. October 2017*, DfE, London, United Kingdom, www.gov.uk/government/uploads/system/uploads/attachment_data/file/650515/SFR53_2017_FINAL.pdf.

DfE (2016), *Apprenticeships Evaluation 2015 – Learners*, A report by IFF Research with the Institute for Employment Research at the University of Warwick, DfE, London, United Kingdom, www.gov.uk/government/uploads/system/uploads/attachment_data/file/562485/Apprenticeships_evaluation_2015_-_Learners.pdf.

European Commission (2013), *Background Paper Mutual Learning Programme. Learning Exchange on 'Apprenticeship Schemes' Vienna, Austria - 7 November 2013*, http://ec.europa.eu/social/main.jsp?langId=en&catId=1073&eventsId=941&furtherEvents=yes&preview=cHJldkVtcGxQb3J0YWwhMjAxMjAyMTVwcmV2aWV3.

Hargreaves, J., J. Stanwick and P. Skujins (2017), *The Changing Nature of Apprenticeships: 1996–2016*, National Centre for Vocational Education Research, Adelaide, Australia.

HM Treasury (2015), *Summer Budget 2015*, www.gov.uk/government/uploads/system/uploads/attachment_data/file/443232/50325_Summer_Budget_15_Web_Accessible.pdf.

House of Commons (2017), *Apprenticeships. Business, Energy and Industrial Strategy and Education, Committees Sub Committee on Education, Skills and the Economy,* www.publications.parliament.uk/pa/cm201617/cmselect/cmese/206/206.pdf.

House of Commons (2016), *Compendium of Apprentice Statistics. Briefing Paper 06113*, http://researchbriefings.parliament.uk/ResearchBriefing/Summary/SN06113#fullreport

HRDF (2016), Malaysia Human Resources Development Fund (HRDF) website, www.hrdf.com.my/ (accessed 8 February 2018).

ILO-World Bank (2013), *Towards a Model Apprenticeship Framework: A Comparative Analysis of National Apprenticeship Systems*, International Labour Organization, International Bank for Reconstruction and Development/The World Bank, Geneva, Switzerland, www.ilo.org/wcmsp5/groups/public/---asia/---ro-bangkok/---sro-new_delhi/documents/publication/wcms_234728.pdf.

Kis, V. (2010), *A Learning for Jobs Review of Ireland 2010,* OECD Reviews of Vocational Education and Training, OECD Publishing, Paris, http://dx.doi.org/10.1787/9789264113848-en.

Knight, B. and T. Karmel (2011), *Apprenticeships and Traineeships in Australia*, Institute for Public Policy Research, London, United Kingdom, www.ippr.org/files/images/media/files/publication/2011/10/rethinking-apprenticeships_3-2_Oct2011_8028.pdf.

Kuczera, M. (2017), "Striking the right balance: Costs and benefits of apprenticeship", *OECD Education Working Papers*, No. 153, OECD Publishing, Paris, http://dx.doi.org/10.1787/995fff01-en.

Lanning, T. (2011), *Why Rethink Apprenticeships? In Rethinking Apprenticeships*, Institute for Public Policy Research, London, United Kingdom.

Musset, P. and S. Field (2013), *A Skills beyond School Review of England*, OECD Reviews of Vocational Education and Training, OECD Publishing, Paris, http://dx.doi.org/10.1787/9789264203594-en.

NCVER (2017a), *Data Slicer: Apprentices and Trainees December 2016*, NCVER, Adelaide, Australia, www.ncver.edu.au/data/data/all-data/data-slicer-apprentices-and-trainees-december-2016.

NCVER (2017b), *Historical Time Series of Apprenticeships and Traineeships in Australia from 1963 to 2017*, NCVER, Adelaide, Australia, www.ncver.edu.au/data/data/all-data/historical-time-series-tables.

NCVER (2011), *Overview of the Australian Apprenticeship and Traineeship System,* www.australianapprenticeships.gov.au/sites/ausapps/files/publication-documents/ncverreport1.pdf.

OECD (2017), *Getting Skills Right*, OECD publishing, Paris, http://dx.doi.org/10.1787/9789264280489-en.

OECD (2016), *Building Skills for All: A Review of England*, www.oecd.org/unitedkingdom/building-skills-for-all-review-of-england.pdf.

Pullen, C. and J. Clifton (2016), *England's Apprenticeships: Assessing the New System*, IPPR, www.ippr.org/files/publications/pdf/Englands_apprenticeships_Aug%202016.pdf?noredirect=1.

Pullen, C. and J. Dromey (2016), *Earning and Learning: Making the Apprenticeship System Work for 16-18 Year Olds*, IPPR, www.ippr.org/files/publications/pdf/earning-and-learning_Nov2016.pdf?noredirect=1.

Richard, D. (2012), *The Richard Review of Apprenticeships,* School for Startups, London, United Kingdom, www.gov.uk/government/uploads/system/uploads/attachment_data/file/34708/richard-review-full.pdf.

Secretariat for Education and Innovation (SERI) Swiss Confederation (2016), *Vocational and Professional Education and Training in Switzerland, Facts and Figures 2016*, www.eda.admin.ch/content/dam/countries/countries-content/canada/en/Vocational-and-professional-education-and-training-switzerland_E.pdf.

Skills Funding Agency (SFA) (2017), "Apprenticeship Funding: Rules for Employers May 2017 to March 2018. Version 1." www.gov.uk/government/publications/apprenticeship-funding-and-performance-management-rules-2017-to-2018.

Wolf, A. (2015), *Fixing a Broken Training System: The Case for an Apprenticeship Levy*, Social Market Foundation, www.smf.co.uk/wp-content/uploads/2015/07/Social-Market-Foundation-Publication-Alison-Wolf-Fixing-A-Broken-Training-System-The-Case-For-An-Apprenticeship-Levy.pdf.

Chapter 2. Promoting and strengthening youth apprenticeships in England

Increasingly, the English apprenticeship system has become numerically dominated by growing numbers of adult apprenticeships. This chapter argues that England could benefit from more youth apprenticeships, strengthened in quality. It explores how youth apprenticeships could be promoted both to employers and young people, by setting the wages and benefits of young apprentices appropriately. The chapter argues that English apprenticeship for young people should provide more general education, including for apprentices that already have Level 2 English and maths qualifications, noting that in comparison to many other countries youth apprentices in England receive less general education. The eligibility of apprentices aged 16-19 for social benefits should also be re-appraised, recognising the need to ensure the attractiveness of apprenticeship.

Introduction: Youth apprenticeships in England

Young people entering the labour market often obtain low quality jobs

Despite low unemployment overall, young people in England often face significant problems when entering the labour market. The UK (numerically dominated by England) unemployment rate for those aged 16-24 is currently 12.5%, slightly down on the previous year. Of these unemployed, about one-third are full-time students seeking part-time work. At the same time, in this age group, about a quarter of those in work are in fact full-time students. But although the figures suggest that some sort of job is open to most young people, there are major issues with the quality of those jobs. Pullen and Dromey (2016) point to many changes in the youth labour market, with more self-employment, more part-time jobs and structures such as zero-hours contracts. Keep (2012) argues that entry level employment is frequently of poor quality, and young workers often have to work on temporary contracts or part-time. Similarly, Shildrick et al., (2012) report that young people leaving school at 16-18 typically get jobs that are low paid, low skilled and insecure. So for many young people, their first jobs are very far from being the first step on a career ladder.

In some apprenticeship systems, youth apprenticeship is more common

Youth apprenticeships are here defined as those catering to young people in their late teens and early twenties; typically these young people have limited relevant work experience. In England, most of these apprenticeships are at Level 2 and 3 corresponding to upper secondary education and training in other countries. England, like some other English-speaking countries has an apprenticeship system numerically dominated by adult apprentices, while in others like Switzerland youth apprenticeships are much more common (see also Figure 1.2). In England, one-quarter of apprenticeship starters are aged 16-18, and a further one-third between 19 and 24. The construction and engineering sectors have the largest share of young apprentices aged 16-18 and 19-24 (84% and 68% respectively) (GOV.UK, 2014). So apprenticeship is no longer synonymous with the school to work transition (Mann, 2016). Some demographic decline in the number of school leavers is currently taking place, and this is affecting trends in the numbers of youth apprenticeships now and in the future. But the modest number of youth apprenticeships (Figure 2.1) may also be reflecting issues in the attractiveness of apprenticeships, both to young people and employers, with young people opting for other forms of education and training, and employers choosing other channels of recruitment.

England's apprenticeship system, serves both adults and youth

For youth apprentices, as with other young people who have completed the comprehensive phase of their schooling at the age of about 16, the need for general education remains significant, as teenagers are still building the knowledge and skills they will need to learn throughout life, to adapt to new career demands, and to play their full role as citizens. Government, in England as in other OECD countries, tends to take a full responsibility for the educational development of these older teenagers, through full funding of most educational programmes, and in other ways, until these young people reach the stage of post-secondary and tertiary education or enter the workforce. For older apprentices, typically incumbent workers, expectations are often different. While government in England and in other OECD countries typically take a close interest in upskilling the workforce and commonly support it in various ways, such upskilling is often seen as something where the responsibility falls more heavily in the shoulders of employers and individuals involved, since these parties are key beneficiaries of the upskilling.

Figure 2.1. Number of apprenticeship starts over time, by age group, in England

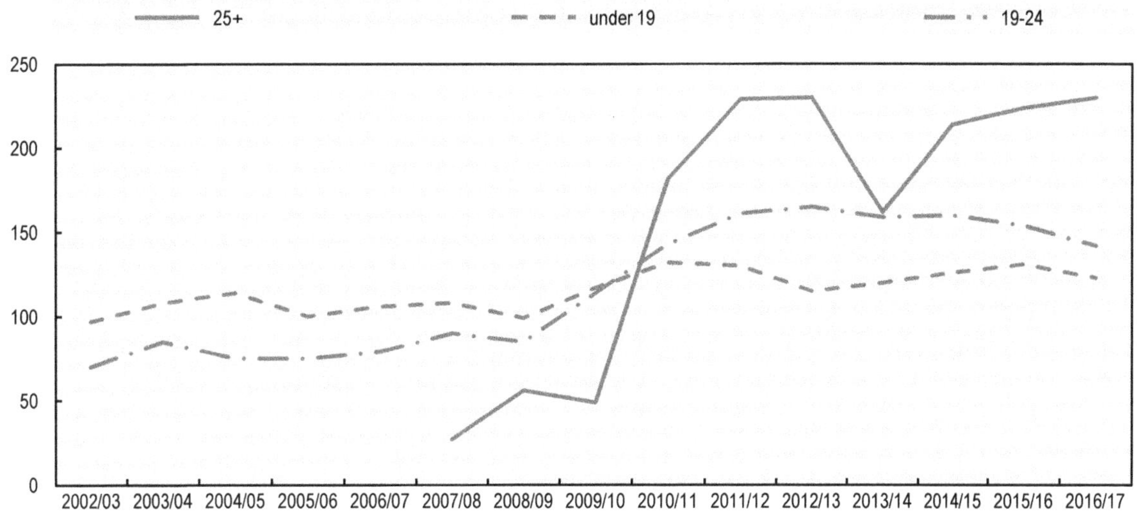

Source: Adapted from Powell, A. (2018), *Apprenticeship Statistics: England,* Briefing *Paper Number 06113,* House of Commons Library, http://researchbriefings.files.parliament.uk/documents/SN06113/SN06113.pdf.

StatLink http://dx.doi.org/10.1787/888933698982

Policy Issue 2.1: Promoting youth apprenticeship

This section looks at how youth apprenticeship might be promoted

While the promotion of youth apprenticeship is already government policy, there are ways in which, within the larger frame of apprenticeship, youth apprenticeships might be given more attention and encouragement. Promotion of youth apprenticeship requires both employer buy-in and an attractive offer for young people. This section therefore looks at how apprentice wages need to balance the interests of employers and the apprentices so as the institution of apprenticeship is attractive to both parties. It then looks at measures that could increase the attractiveness of apprenticeships to young people, such as better benefits for young apprentices. It then looks at how to increase benefits from apprenticeships for young apprentices.

Challenge: Transition from school to work is hard for some young people in England

In England, many young people experience a difficult transition from school to work

In 2012 in England, only 70% of 16-19 year-olds were participating in education or training leading to a formal qualification, compared to nearly universal participation in, for example, the Czech Republic, Poland, Estonia and the Netherlands (OECD, 2016, Table A2.1). This reflects low participation rates among older teenagers in England, with participation in full or part-time education at 90% among 16-year-olds, falling to only 56% for 18-year-olds in 2013 (OECD 2016a; DfE, 2015c). Many learners do not complete the 16-18 phase of education, with many dropping out from programmes leading to Level 2 qualifications (Pullen and Dromey, 2016). In the United Kingdom, 9% of young people (15-19 year-olds) are not in employment, education and training, more than in many OECD countries (OECD, 2018). For young people at risk, it follows that there are good reasons for looking to apprenticeships and pre-apprenticeships as a means of facilitating completion of Level 2/3 qualifications and transition to skilled jobs. The equity issues are further addressed in Chapter 6.

The impact of new reforms on youth apprenticeship is uncertain

Prior to the introduction of the levy, many employers were, in principle, paying around half the cost of the off-the-job training for older apprentices – although in practice local cross-subsidies probably reduced the impact of this funding arrangement. Now the levy is in place, (and setting aside the levy payments themselves) employers will now only have to pay a maximum of 10% (and often nothing) for the-off-the job training of their apprentices. This may trigger a further acceleration in the growth of adult apprenticeships – perhaps displacing some young apprentices. To balance this additional support for adult apprenticeships, the government has exempted employers who offer apprenticeships to those who are 25 or younger from payment of National Insurance. Other measures encouraging provision of apprenticeships to youth include a grant of GBP 1 000 to employers taking on apprentices aged 16-18 (and to the training providers), and a lower apprentice wage in the case of young apprentices (Powell, 2017). The net effect of all these changes on youth apprenticeships is as yet unclear.

Apprentices under 19 are not eligible for benefits available to their peers in full-time education

In England, young people who become apprentices lose some benefits which they would retain if they remained in full-time education. Parents are eligible for Child Benefit, Child Tax Credit and Universal Credit if their child is aged 16-19 and is in full-time education and training other than higher education. Those in paid work, including apprentices, are not eligible (GOV.UK, 2018). The 2017 conservative election manifesto proposes to offer discounted bus and train travel for apprentices (Conservative Party, 2017).

Policy pointer 2.1: Promoting youth apprenticeships

In the light of a significant challenge of transitioning young people with poor school attainment into good quality jobs, the government should seek an expansion of quality youth apprenticeships, as in other countries, where such apprenticeships play a major role.

Options include:

- Evaluate the impact of the existing wage setting on provision of apprenticeship by employers in different sectors, and on the uptake of apprenticeships by individuals across different age groups.
- Explore whether the threshold effect induced by a sharp wage increases when an apprentice turns 19 or completes the first year of apprenticeship may prevent employers from providing longer apprenticeships.
- Ensure that where youth apprentice wages are low, that they are balanced by extensive benefits to the young apprentice, in terms of the quality of the learning opportunities with the employer, to avoid exploitation of youth apprentices as unskilled labour (as also argued in Chapter 3).
- In recognition of their status as a learner (as well as a worker), apprentices aged 16-19 (and their families) should be eligible for social benefits sufficiently attractive to allow youth apprenticeship to compete fairly, and without any bias in connection with social background, with other educational programmes for 16-19 year-olds.

- In line with other targets for apprenticeship, set up a target for an expansion of youth apprenticeships.

Analysis: Outcomes from apprenticeships

Evidence shows that apprenticeships smooth transition of young people to the labour market

Apprenticeships systematically blend education and training provided in schools and in work places, facilitating the transition of young people from school to work. Across countries, there is evidence that graduate apprentices have better labour market chances in terms of duration of job search, unemployment spells and wages than those who choose another type of upper secondary education (Bratberg and Nilsen, 1998; van der Klaauw et al., 2004; European Commission, 2013).

Individual and social outcomes from youth apprenticeship in the United Kingdom are positive

A study evaluating outcomes from apprenticeship in the United Kingdom (Level 2 and 3) between 1996 and 2004/2005 showed that apprenticeship was associated with a positive wage premium when compared with qualifications at a lower level (Level 1 and 2 respectively) and other vocational qualifications of similar level. The study also demonstrated that investment in apprenticeship was beneficial from the government point of view (McIntosh, 2007). These results refer mainly to youth apprenticeships as during the reference period there were relatively few apprentices above the age of 25 (see Figure 2.1).

Analysis: Apprentice wages

In some countries, apprentice wages increase gradually over the course of a 3- to 4-year apprenticeship

Other things being equal, employers might prefer to train adults with relevant work experience than young school leavers, as adults require less training and their productivity will be higher at the outset. On the other hand, apprentice wages are typically lower for young people, and these wages are usually the main component of costs to employers. Table 2.1 shows how the apprentice wage compares to the skilled worker wage, and the contribution of wage costs to total apprenticeship costs across countries. In other countries, apprentice wages commonly increase gradually but substantially during a 3- to 4-year apprenticeship, reflecting increasing skills and productivity. For example, in Austria, an apprentice in the metal processing industry earns EUR 550 per month in the first year, EUR 740 in the second year, EUR 1 010 in the third year, and EUR 1 360 in the fourth year (European Commission, 2013). For a young apprentice plasterer (under 21) in Australia, the hourly rate in 2013 was AUD 10 in the first year, just under AUD 12 in the second year, around AUD 16 in year three, and around AUD 19 in their final fourth year (CFMEU Construction, 2010).

Table 2.1. Apprentice wages across countries

	What is the apprentice wage, as compared to the skilled worker's wage?	What is the share of the apprentice wage cost in the total cost of the apprenticeship programme?
Austria	On average 50% of the skilled worker wage.	57% of total costs in the first year and 72% in the third year of the apprenticeship
Germany	25-33% of the skilled worker wage, depending on the year of the programme.	Around 62%
Norway	30-80% of the skilled worker wage, depending on the year of the programme.	Information not available
Switzerland	On average 20% of the skilled worker wage, depending on the year of the programme.	Around 50%

Source: Kuczera M. (2017), "Striking the right balance. Costs and benefits of apprenticeships", *OECD Education Working Papers*, No. 153, http://dx.doi.org/10.1787/995fff01-en.

In England, apprenticeships may involve a sharp wage increase after 12 months

In England an apprentice earns between 50% and 60% of the skilled worker wage but this average hides large variations. In 2011 apprentices under 19 earned approximately 32% of the fully qualified rate, while those aged 19-24 earned 49% (Conlon et al., 2013). The prevailing youth apprentice wage in England is thus close to that of their Austrian counterparts, but above that of their counterparts in Germany and Switzerland. In England, according to the law, the minimum wage of apprentices aged under 19, and those aged 19 or over in the first year of their apprenticeships amounts to 47% of the national minimum wage (GOV.UK, 2017a). Turning 19 or completing the first year of an apprenticeship trigger a substantial increase in an apprentice's wage, if the apprentice is paid the legal minimum. For example, the legal minimum wage of an apprentice who started on a programme at the age of 18 will increase in the second year by 60%. This sharp increase may encourage employers to provide apprenticeships that do not greatly exceed one year in length. Around one-third of apprenticeships may be concerned as the recent apprentice pay survey shows that the rate of non-compliance with the minimum wage in the second year of apprenticeships among those 19-20 year-olds is 32% (BEIS, 2017). If these employers had to comply with the legal requirements, which they definitely should, they may opt for an apprenticeship not exceeding one year.

In some cases, employers may be relatively indifferent to the apprentice wage

Figure 2.2 shows how apprentice wages and productivity may change over the course of an apprenticeship in sectors where employers invest in apprenticeship to realise long-term benefits. It illustrates the case where an increase in apprentice productivity, resulting from the training, does not compensate for the costs related to wages by the end of apprenticeship – the employers therefore bear net costs during the apprenticeship, because they see it as a longer-term investment in the skills of their workforce. Many of these employers already pay youth apprentices above the minimum required wage and would be unaffected by a drop in the apprentice minimum wage. The costs illustrated only include apprentice wages, but if other in-kind resource costs to the employer were included, such as the cost of the supervision of apprentices, the net employer costs would be even larger. It is difficult to estimate exactly how many apprenticeships fall in this category of youth apprenticeships leading to long-term benefits. But 90% of 16-18 year-olds and 60% of 19-24 year-olds apprentices were recruited externally (Department for Education 2016), typically to meet longer-term skills needs. In some sectors this type of apprenticeship is more common than in others. Hogarth, Gambin, and Winterbotham (2012) report that, in the engineering and construction sector, nearly all interviewed employers offered apprenticeships to meet their future skills needs. Apprenticeship positions were mainly offered, at wages above the minima, to young people between 16 and 24 who had recently completed full-time education.

Figure 2.2. Comparison of apprentice wages and productivity in an engineering and construction company in the United Kingdom (England)

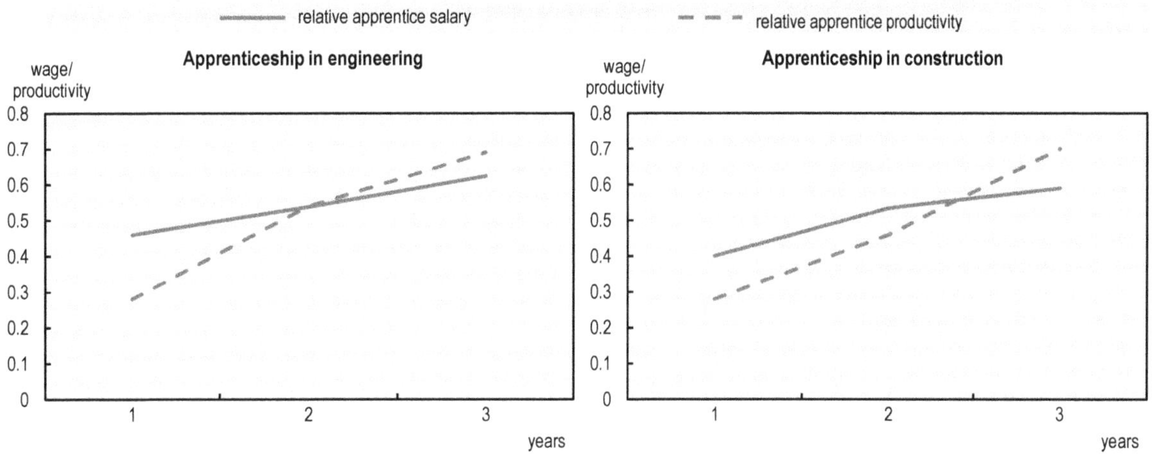

Note: Relative apprentice wage = apprentice wage/skilled worker wage. Relative apprentice productivity = apprentice productivity/skilled worker productivity.
Source: Adapted from Hogarth, T., L. Gambin, and M. Winterbotham (2012), "Employer investment in apprenticeships and workplace learning: The fifth net benefits of training to employers study", *BIS research paper*, number 67, www.gov.uk/government/publications/employer-investment-in-apprenticeships-and-workplace-learning-the-fifth-net-benefits-of-training-to-employers-study.

StatLink http://dx.doi.org/10.1787/888933699001

Employers who are not able to retain apprenticeship graduates may be more responsive to wage levels

Employers, who cannot count on recruiting or retaining apprenticeship graduates will only offer apprenticeships if they are able to break even by the end of the programme (for more information on costs and benefits from apprenticeships see for example Muehlemann, 2016 and Kuczera, 2017). Costs and benefits analysis of apprenticeship carried out in Switzerland shows that this is possible if employers use apprentices in productive work, while paying them below the regular wage (Muehlemann, 2016). In these circumstances, employers may be very sensitive to change in youth apprenticeship minimum wages. However, a lower apprentice wage increases the opportunity cost for apprentices. Lower wages would therefore need to be matched with standards and regulations ensuring a high-quality apprenticeship and making the investment worthwhile.

Wage setting – at which level?

Costs and benefits of apprenticeships to employers, and therefore reasons why employers provide apprenticeships, vary across companies and sectors. For example, in England employers in construction and engineering are more likely to provide apprenticeships to young people with recruitment benefits in mind. Conversely, in the health and retail sectors employers often offer apprenticeships to incumbent workers. Apprentices in these sectors also tend to be older (Hogarth, Gambin and Winterbotham, 2012; DfE, 2016). As a result the costs and benefits structure and so the impact of the minimum apprentice wage on apprenticeship provision would be very different across sectors. To reflect this variation across sectors in many countries the minimum apprentice wage and its progression through the programme duration is set by sectors. This is different from the English approach where the minimum wage is defined nationally. Table 2.2 compares wage-setting arrangements across countries.

Table 2.2. How the minimum apprentice wage is determined

	Level at which the minimum apprentice wage is determined
Australia	Sectors at national and regional level; in some cases it is up to individual companies
Austria	Sectors at regional level
Denmark	Sectors
England (UK)	National
Germany	Sectors at regional level
Netherlands	Sectors
Norway	Sectors at national level
Scotland	National
Switzerland	Unregulated but in practice sectoral/industry bodies provide recommendations on the wage level that are observed by individual employers

Note: Apprentice wages can vary widely across sectors and tend to increase over the duration of the apprenticeship programme.
Source: Kuczera M. (2017), "Striking the right balance. Costs and benefits of apprenticeships", *OECD Education Working Papers*, No. 153, http://dx.doi.org/10.1787/995fff01-en.

Young apprentices are more likely to accept lower wages if they expect good returns later

Wage setting should also reflect what apprentices are willing to work for – the reservation wage. Younger individuals will typically have a lower apprentice reservation wage as, through an apprenticeship, they can expect to recoup the investment in their own skills over a lifetime. They may also have low short-term costs as many still live with their parents. But the apprenticeship still needs to provide sufficiently attractive longer-term labour market returns, meaning a high-quality apprenticeship. So, youth apprenticeships should provide participants with solid basic skills and transferable occupational skills.

Older apprentices have a higher reservation wage

Adult apprentices typically have higher expectations in terms of the apprentice wage. They often have families to support, and the alternative to apprenticeship is often a job with an unskilled wage. For these reasons apprentice wages tend to be higher for older apprentices in England and other countries. To support older apprentices, other countries provide grants and subsidies to this population. In Germany, apprentices over 25 may receive financial support for education expenses, travel, child care, tutoring, and a subsistence allowance during the training. In Switzerland, adult apprentices earn around two-thirds of the unskilled worker wage, compared to one-fifth for younger apprentices. All those under 35 can apply for a scholarship of a maximum CHF 12 000 per year (equivalent to 2.5 times the median monthly wage of an unskilled worker). Additional financial assistance is available to those who are unemployed. In Canada the apprentice wage starts at around 50% of the skilled worker wage and the Canadian government offers apprentices one-off grants of up to CAD 4 000 (the minimum average hourly wage in Canada is CAD 11.43) (Muehlemann, forthcoming). While these measures potentially increase the participation of older adults in apprenticeships, a robust evaluation of their impact is lacking. There is some evidence that the cost of participation in apprenticeships may be unacceptably high for some potential adult apprentices in England (Young Women's Trust, 2017). Given that one-third of older apprentices do not receive the legal minimum apprentice wage it is vital to ensure that employers comply with the legal pay requirements. To support adult learners, the government may also explore introduction of other measures in line with other countries' experience, as discussed above.

Regulation is needed to ensure that adult and other apprentices have suitable job roles

When employers provide apprenticeships mainly to benefit from the productive work of apprentices in unskilled roles, they will have less incentive to invest in training and skills development of their apprentices. In this context it is important to ensure apprentices receive training in the work place, preparing them for skilled jobs, alongside contributing to productive work. Regulation is therefore needed to ensure that the apprenticeship is of good quality and to prevent exploitation. Chapter 3 will argue that regulations and standards on the workplace training provided by employers would help to prevent employers from using apprentices solely as unskilled labour.

Benefits equivalent to those received by other students would encourage youth apprenticeship

In England, young apprentices lose the benefits for which other students under 19 are eligible. The English approach contrasts with practices in other countries (Box 2.1) where apprentices retain many of the benefits full-time students are eligible for, and at the same time receive an apprentice wage from the employer. This means that in England, while young apprentices receiving apprentice wages are typically better off than their student counterparts, and they earn more than their parents/families would receive in benefits, they are less generously treated in respect of benefits than their apprentice counterparts in some other countries. This point is relevant to any assessment of the prevalence and status of apprenticeship in England in comparison with other countries.

Box 2.1. Social benefits available to apprentices

In **Austria**, parents with children below 18, and those with children in training for an occupation or studying at the post-secondary level are eligible for family allowances. The Austrian Government also pays for most of the costs incurred for travel to school or the training location as well as educational material for children and young people enrolled in schools or undergoing training as apprentices.

In **Australia** low-income 18-24 year-olds in full-time education and 16-24 year-olds in Australian Apprenticeships can benefit from income support through the Youth Allowance Student Payment.

In **the Netherlands**, students and apprentices under the age of 18 receive free education and training and their parents remain eligible for child benefits. But apprentices, unlike other vocational students, are not entitled to reductions in public transport costs.

Source: Austria: HELP.gv.at (2018), Additional benefits and support for parents www.help.gv.at/Portal.Node/hlpd/public/content/143/Seite.1430900.html; Australia: OECD (2016b), *Investing in Youth: Australia*, OECD Publishing, Paris, http://dx.doi.org/10.1787/9789264257498-en; Australian Government Department of Human Services (2018), Youth allowance, www.humanservices.gov.au/customer/services/centrelink/youth-allowance; Australian Government (2018), Family assistance guide, 1.1.F.60 Full-time secondary study (FTB), http://guides.dss.gov.au/family-assistance-guide/1/1/f/60; Australian Government Department of Social Services (2018), Student payments, www.dss.gov.au/our-responsibilities/families-and-children/programmes-services/student-payments; Netherlands: Government of the Netherlands (2018), Kosten mbo opleiding, www.rijksoverheid.nl/onderwerpen/middelbaar-beroepsonderwijs/inhoud/kosten-mbo-opleiding.

Policy issue 2.2: Strengthening the general education component of youth apprenticeship

This section argues that young apprentices in England would benefit from stronger general education, including better basic skills, and discusses how this could be achieved.

Challenge: Increasing general education in youth apprenticeships leading to stronger basic skills

The 2012 Survey of Adult Skills showed young people in England had low basic skills

Young people in England perform less well on the basic skills of literacy and numeracy than their peers in many other OECD countries. According to the Survey of Adult Skills, England has one of the largest shares of 16-24 year-olds with weak basic skills among the participating countries, and those with vocational qualifications are particularly at risk (OECD, 2016a).

Requirements for English and maths among apprentices have been increased

To ensure all young people have adequate maths and English, the government now requires all young people, including apprentices, to pursue at least Level 2 qualifications in mathematics and English (at least GCSE C or equivalent),[1] and pays the provider GBP 471 for delivery of the relevant qualification. In 2014 around half apprentices under 25 received education and training in basic skills during their working hours in England (BIS 2014, pp 46). The new reformed vocational education and training (VET) system is intended to improve basic skills among young people by introducing a common core of more general education in vocational strands. As well as good literacy and numeracy, everyone will be provided with the essential set of digital skills necessary to succeed in the modern workplace (BIS, 2016, pp. 24). Precise requirements and how they will apply to young apprentices are not entirely clear as yet.

General education is an important part of vocational education and training

General education is defined here as leading to generic knowledge and skills, not directly relevant to a specific occupation and applicable in most contexts of work and life. It would include numeracy, literacy, science, social studies and civic education. General education is part of occupational training: a well-qualified electrician needs to be familiar with basic mathematical and physical laws. General education does not necessarily require classroom settings, and can take place in informal environments and the workplace. Since informal learning is difficult to quantify, this report compares the amount of formal general education received by apprentices as part of their programmes in different countries, focusing on the upper secondary level (Level 2 and 3 in England).

In other countries apprentices normally receive more general education than in England

In Switzerland, all apprentices receive 2.5 hours per week of teaching in the official language, communication, civic education (including some applied mathematics) and 45 minutes of physical education (e.g. see programme for kitchen employees (BBZ Biel Küchenangestellte/r, n.d.). This adds up to 120 hours of basic skills education and sport per year – so approaching 400 hours over a 3-year apprenticeship (Confédération Suisse, 2006). Some programmes are more demanding: an apprenticeship in clock making (in addition to the mandatory 2.5 hours block) requires 90 minutes in mathematics and 45 minutes in informatics per week in the 1st year; 45 minutes in mathematics and 45 minutes in physics in the 2nd year; and 45 minutes in physics in the third year (BBZ Biel Horloger, n.d.). In Germany, apprentices receive 160 hours annually of general education, and this time is divided among subjects such as German, English, sports, and economics or social science (Hoeckel and Schwartz, 2010). In Norway, most apprentices spend the first two years of their apprenticeship in full-time school education before moving to a work placement for the remaining two years of their apprenticeship. During the two school-based years apprentices must pursue 588 hours of basic education including Norwegian (or other official language), mathematics, English, science and physical education (Norwegian Directorate for Education and Training, 2011). In addition to general education, apprentices in the three countries also receive education and training in occupation-specific subjects during their off-the-job education. Conversely, in Australia, the employer-led training packages which define apprenticeships contain relatively limited amount of general education, and for that reason have been criticised as inadequate (see Knight and Karmel, 2011).

Apprentices in England receive much less general education than their peers in other countries

Acquisition of a Level 2 qualification in maths or in English typically involves 45 guided learning hours (e.g. Pearson, 2017 and NCFE, n.d.). Assuming guided learning hours are equivalent to learning time, this implies that an apprentice spends roughly one hour per week on these subjects over a period of a year if she or he does not meet the minimum requirements in English or maths, or two hours per week if she or he does not meet requirements in either subject. This adds up to around 50-100 hours of general education focused on maths and literacy, compared with around 400 hours mandatory education (covering a wide range of subjects) for apprenticeships in the countries mentioned. Some English apprentices will receive more general education if that is what is required by the standard for the specific apprenticeships, but this depends entirely on the standard. These are large differences, recognising that, as explained earlier, the starting point for a young English apprentice will often be numeracy and literacy levels below those of other countries.

General education should not merely be remedial, it also supports progression to further study

Basic skills teaching is not mandatory for young people who already have Level 2 English and maths or higher. While some basic skills may be implicit in individual apprenticeship standards, according to the select committee report, some standards provide a worryingly narrow set of skills (House of Commons, 2017). Many standards do not require classroom teaching in basic skills other than those directly related to the specific occupational skills (see GOV.UK, 2017b). Given the aspiration to develop higher-level apprenticeships, and provide all apprentices with the kind of core academic skills that will facilitate further studies, more general education will be needed. It is not enough, as at present, to define a remedial numeracy and literacy module for those lacking the relevant prior school qualifications. Pullen and Dromey (2016) also argue that insufficient general education is included in youth apprenticeships to support progression to further study, and in comparison with strong European apprenticeship systems. On that basis, they argue that Level 2 apprenticeships for 16-18 year-olds should be restructured as pre-apprenticeship programmes that would include more general education.

This raises a broader issue of the principles defining apprenticeship standards

In England the apprenticeship standards that will drive the content of the 20% of programme duration required for training (mainly off-the-job) are developed by employers. This makes excellent sense, but it is subject to a limitation that has not been fully addressed in England. While employers will be interested in relevant occupational skills it is not realistic to expect them to take a close interest in general education, including numeracy, literacy and foreign languages. This is because these skills improve the employment opportunities of individuals and increase the chances of employees finding jobs elsewhere. In Austria, Denmark Germany, Switzerland and Norway by contrast, while employers take the lead in defining work-based learning requirements, and the core competences required for the target profession, the curriculum for off-the-job education and training (often also approximating to 20% of programme duration) is developed primarily by government and the education authorities in collaboration with social partners, and is therefore deliberately designed, in terms of its governance, to address the broader educational requirements of young apprentices.

Policy pointer 2.2: Giving attention to wider education in youth apprenticeship

The broader education of young apprentices, including numeracy, literacy and digital skills, is extremely important. While more young people have weak numeracy and literacy skills in England than in many other countries, young apprentices receive less general education than their apprentice counterparts in many other countries. New requirements for the study of maths and English among apprentices are to be welcomed, but they do not go far enough. They do not address the needs for higher-level literacy and numeracy skills, and wider education, so as to support higher-level apprenticeships and pathways to further study.

- In the long run, all apprenticeships should provide more general education, including for apprentices that already have Level 2 English and maths qualifications. More demanding requirements may be necessary for youth apprenticeships, for example through a pre-apprenticeship programme linked to a technical qualification, with general education as a precursor to a full apprenticeship. This would be consistent with the government's broader strategy for post-16 education.

Analysis: Apprenticeships conveying strong basic skills are associated with better outcomes

Basic skills provided early on lead to many benefits

There is solid evidence showing that good numeracy and literacy skills developed early on in life yield positive labour market and social outcomes (OECD, 2013). This is because learning is a dynamic process, in which successive stages depend on skills acquired previously (Heckman, 2008). In many countries with strong apprenticeship systems[2] young people may choose apprenticeship when they reach upper secondary level (Level 2 or 3 in the United Kingdom) at around the age of 16. Often, this level of education is seen as an educational minimum, and for this reason apprenticeships often include some of the same type of education received by their peers in full-time school education and training. This will commonly include numeracy, literacy and other generic skills, taught off-the-job in a vocational school or an equivalent institution.

Strong basic skills increase the actual and perceived value of apprenticeships

Recent research shows that young people in England associate apprenticeships with limited future career choices and poor opportunities for academic progression (e.g. Mann, 2016). For apprenticeship to be attractive to young people, it should lead to outcomes that are at least as good as those arising from alternative routes that would have an equivalent 'cost' to the student. The outcomes can be measured in terms of wages, employment opportunities in short and long term, and opportunities to continue in education and training. All these outcomes are positively associated with basic skills, and in England, the labour market returns to numeracy and literacy skills are greater than in many other countries (OECD, 2013). For high ability students, apprenticeship that also includes a strong element of the core academic skills, including numeracy and literacy, and that therefore support further learning, will be particularly attractive. The capacity of apprenticeship to attract high ability young people will in turn encourage employers to offer apprenticeships. A strengthened element of general education would therefore allow apprenticeship not only to stand comparison with high-quality apprenticeships in other countries, but would also compete well with other offers, including post-GCSE options such as A-levels, the new T-levels and other forms of full-time post-secondary education.

Apprenticeships can help to transition young people with weak basic skills through to completion

For those apprentices with the weakest basic skills, there is a substantial risk of dropout. Chapter 6 looks at the arrangements made by other countries to address this challenge, including pre-apprenticeship programmes that prepare young people to enter full apprenticeships, targeted support for those at risk during their apprenticeship, including additional support for numeracy and literacy, and special types of apprenticeship adapted to those with the weakest basic skills. All these measures are very relevant to English apprenticeship. But effective general education, with significant attention to basic skills, should be very much part of this effort.

Analysis: Funding the general education component of apprenticeships

In some other countries government funds the general education component of apprenticeship

In apprenticeship systems in continental European countries apprentices typically receive general education, including basic skills, as well as some more theoretical training in their target occupation, off-the-job in a vocational school or college. Funding arrangements often depend on the age of participants and the level of qualification. Off-the-job education in apprenticeship programmes for young people that lead to upper secondary qualifications is typically fully funded by public authorities. Off-the-job education for apprentices at post-secondary level and for older individuals sometimes involves fees. For example, in the Netherlands, while apprentices who are below the age of 18 receive their education and training for free, those who are 18 and above must pay tuition or course fees, which are set every year by the government (Ministerie van Onderwijs, 2011).

In England, also general education for apprentices is funded by government

Like other countries, in England, Level 2 English and maths is fully funded by the government, the provider receiving GBP 471 for delivery of the relevant qualification. If more general education, including basic skills, were to be introduced in all youth apprenticeship programmes at Levels 2 and 3 (the equivalent of upper secondary education elsewhere) the government would need to cover the cost. State funding would be justified on the grounds of efficiency as early investment in skills yields larger benefits than interventions later in life and on the grounds of equity, if other comparable qualifications provided in public institutions, such as technical education and A-levels, are provided free of charge. It would also be consistent with the practice in other countries in respect of state-funded off-the-job education of apprentices.

An increase in general education requirements for apprentices would increase the time which employers would need to release apprentices

An increase in general education requirements would add to the existing cost to employers of releasing apprentices for training for 20% of their time. For example, currently an additional 90 minutes of basic skills per week is provided to apprentices without Level 2 English and maths, thus increasing the proportion of off-the-job training time to around 24%. This is consistent with arrangements encountered in other countries where apprentices spend between 25-30% of their time off-the-job (see Table 1.1). But further increases in the off-the-job time or extension of basic skills teaching to all youth apprenticeships (including those who already have Level 2 English and maths) might well meet resistance from employers in England who since April 2017 have had to pay the apprenticeship levy. This could lead to fewer employers offering apprenticeships to young people.

But this additional cost is offset by the subsidy received by employers who provide apprenticeship to those under 19

The employer cost of taking on young apprentices is reduced by a subsidy of GBP 1 000 offered to employers when they take on 16-18 year-olds, (or 19-24 year-olds who are in care or who have an education and health care plan). Employers are free to direct some or all this additional incentive payment to providers should they wish (DfE, 2017). If the scheme is to be preserved in the future this additional money could cover the cost of the apprentice wage while apprentices are off-the-job in English, maths and other general education classes.

Provision of basic skills prior to starting on apprenticeships may be another option

Alternatively, apprenticeship could be organised in blocks, linking apprenticeship to new planned vocational/technical education qualifications and apprenticeships (BIS, 2016). Students would first receive school-based education, which would formally be in pursuit of a technical qualification rather than defined as an apprenticeship, followed by an apprenticeship involving work placement with a company and off-the-job education as currently defined in standards. This would follow the Norwegian model of apprenticeship. The employer would therefore not incur any costs associated with the school-based education and training. In this model young people would be able to acquire relevant information about available apprenticeship options that would inform their career choice while still in school. Evidence shows that currently career information in schools in England is skewed towards academic options (Mann and Huddleston, 2016; Ali, 2016). This proposal is in some ways similar to the policy option proposed by Chapter 6 of this report, and to the IPPR (Pullen and Dromey, 2016) proposal that lower level apprenticeships for 16-18 year-olds should be replaced by a pre-apprenticeship programme, including a qualification, with a stronger element of general education. This chapter argues that this model, involving a period of general education and some occupational training, followed by a period of work-based learning with the company, can also be successfully applied in higher-level qualifications.

Notes

[1] Those with learning difficulties and disabilities will be exempted from this requirement.

[2] Countries with large apprenticeship systems are those with at least 10% of the young people enrolled in apprenticeship as shown in Figure 1.1.

References

Ali, A. (2017), "A-level results: UK education system only prepares students for exams and not careers, survey finds", *The Independent*, 7 August 2017, www.independent.co.uk/student/career-planning/apprenticeships/a-level-results-2016-going-to-university-benefits-of-apprenticeships-a7195201.html.

BBZ Biel (n.d), *Küchenangestellte/r EBA*, www.bbz-biel.ch/berufs-lehre/berufe/kuechenangestellter/.

BBZ Biel (n.d), *Horloger/Industrie CFC*, www.cfp-bienne.ch/fr/apprentissage/professions/horloger-industrie.

BIS (Department of Business, Innovation and Skills) (2014), "Apprenticeships evaluation: Learner survey", *BIS Research Paper*, No. 205, www.gov.uk/government/publications/apprenticeships-evaluation-learner-survey-2014.

BIS (2016), Post 16 Skills Plan, www.gov.uk/government/uploads/system/uploads/attachment_data/file/536068/56259_Cm_9280_print.pdf.

BEIS (Department for Business, Energy and Industrial Strategy) (2017), "Apprenticeship pay survey 2016: Great Britain", *BEIS Research Paper*, No. 15, www.gov.uk/government/uploads/system/uploads/attachment_data/file/630070/apprenticeship-pay-survey-2016-report-gb.pdf.

Bratberg, E. and Ø. Nilsen (1998), "Transition from school to work: Search time and job duration", *IZA Discussion Paper*, No. 27, Institute for the Study of Labor (IZA), https://ideas.repec.org/p/iza/izadps/dp27.html.

CFMEU Construction (2010), *Apprentices Rates of Pay for Apprentices Working for an Incorporated Employer That Is Covered by the Building and Construction General on-Site Award 2010*, www.cfmeunsw.asn.au/sites/cfmeunsw.asn.au/files/downloads/award/apprentice-wage-sheet-july-2013.pdf.

Christoffels, I., J. Cuppen and S. Vrielink (2016), "Verzameling notities over de daling van de bbl en praktijkleren - Rapport - Rijksoverheid.nl", Rapport ECBO, MOOZ, www.rijksoverheid.nl/documenten/rapporten/2016/10/18/verzameling-notities-over-de-daling-van-de-bbl-en-praktijkleren.

Confédération Suisse (2006), "412.101.241 Ordonnance du SEFRI du 27 avril 2006 concernant les conditions minimales relatives à la culture générale dans la formation professionnelle initiale du 27 avril 2006", www.admin.ch/opc/fr/classified-compilation/20061526/index.html.

Conlon, G., et al. (2013), *An International Comparison of Apprentice Pay: Final Report*, LE London Economics, www.gov.uk/government/uploads/system/uploads/attachment_data/file/289425/London_Economics_Apprentice_Pay_FINAL.pdf.

Conservative Party (2017), *The Conversative and Unionist Party Manifesto 2017*, https://s3-eu-west-1.amazonaws.com/2017-manifestos/Conservative+Manifesto+2017.pdf.

DfE (Department for Education) (2017), *Apprenticeship Funding: How it Works*, www.gov.uk/government/publications/apprenticeship-levy-how-it-will-work/apprenticeship-levy-how-it-will-work.

DfE (Department for Education) (2016), *Apprenticeships Evaluation 2015 - Learners,* A report by IFF Research, with the Institute for Employment Research at the University of Warwick, DfE, London, United Kingdom, www.gov.uk/government/uploads/system/uploads/attachment_data/file/562485/Apprenticeships_evaluation_2015_-_Learners.pdf.

European Commission (2013), *Background Paper Mutual Learning Programme. Learning Exchange on 'Apprenticeship Schemes' Vienna, Austria - 7 November 2013*, http://ec.europa.eu/social/main.jsp?langId=en&catId=1073&eventsId=941&furtherEvents=yes&preview=cHJldkVtcGxQb3J0YWwhMjAxMjAyMTVwcmV2aWV3.

EU Commission (2013), *The Effectiveness and Costs-Benefits of Apprenticeships: Results of the Quantitative Analysis.*

GOV.UK (2018), "Child Benefit when your child turns 16", www.gov.uk/child-benefit-16-19 (accessed 2 February 2018).

GOV.UK (2017a), “National minimum wage and national living wage rates”, www.gov.uk/national-minimum-wage-rates.

GOV.UK (2017b), “Guidance. Search for apprenticeship standards”, www.gov.uk/guidance/search-for-apprenticeship-standards#adult-care-standards.

GOV.UK (2014), “Statistical data set: FE data library: apprenticeships”, www.gov.uk/government/statistical-data-sets/fe-data-library-apprenticeships.

Heckman, J. (2008), “Schools, skills, and synapses”, *Economic Inquiry,* Vol. 46/3, pp. 289–324, http://dx.doi.org/10.1111/j.1465-7295.2008.00163.x.

Hoeckel, K. and R. Schwartz (2010), *OECD Reviews of Vocational Education and Training: A Learning for Jobs Review of Germany 2010*, OECD Publishing, Paris, http://dx.doi.org/10.1787/9789264113800-en.

Knight, B. and T. Karmel (2011), *Apprenticeships and Traineeships in Australia*, Institute for Public Policy Research, London, www.ippr.org/files/images/media/files/publication/2011/10/rethinking-apprenticeships_3-2_Oct2011_8028.pdf.

Kuczera M. (2017) “Striking the right balance: Costs and benefits of apprenticeship”, *OECD Education Working Papers*, No. 153, OECD Publishing, Paris. http://dx.doi.org/10.1787/995fff01-en.

Mann A. (2016), "Young people in apprenticeships", in D. Way (ed.) (2016), *A Race to the Top: Achieving Three Million More Apprenticeships by 2020,* Winchester University Press.

Mann A. and P. Huddleston (2017), “School and the twenty-first century labour market: perspective on structural challenges”, *British Journal of Guidance & Counselling*, Vol. 45/2, pp.208–18, https://doi.org/10.1080/03069885.2016.1266440.

Ministerie van Onderwijs, Cultuur en Wetenschap (2011), “Secondary vocational education (MBO) - Secondary vocational education (MBO) and higher education - Government.nl.” Onderwerp, www.government.nl/topics/secondary-vocational-education-mbo-and-higher-education/contents/secondary-vocational-education-mbo.

Muehlemann S. (forthcoming), “Apprenticeship training for adults: theoretical considerations and empirical evidence for selected OECD member countries".

Mühlemann, S. (2016), "The cost and benefits of work-based learning", *OECD Education Working Papers*, No. 143, OECD Publishing, Paris, http://dx.doi.org/10.1787/5jlpl4s6g0zv-en.

NCFE (n.d.), *NCFE Functional Skills. Qualifications in Maths*, www.ncfe.org.uk/media/822739/maths-summary-sheet.pdf.

Norwegian Directorate for Education and Training (2011), Fag- og timefordelingen i grunnopplæringen – Kunnskapsløftet , www.udir.no/Upload/Rundskriv/2011/Udir-1-2011-Fag-og-timefordeling_des2011.pdf.

OECD (2018), Youth not in employment, education or training (NEET) (indicator), http://dx.doi.org/10.1787/72d1033a-en (accessed on 1 March 2018).

OECD (2016a), *Building Skills for All: A Review of England Policy Insights from the Survey of Adult Skills*, Paris, www.oecd.org/edu/skills-beyond-school/building-skills-for-all-review-of-england.pdf.

OECD (2016b), *Investing in Youth: Australia*, OECD Publishing, Paris, http://dx.doi.org/10.1787/9789264257498-en.

OECD (2013), *OECD Skills Outlook 2013: First Results from the Survey of Adult Skills*, OECD Publishing, Paris, http://dx.doi.org/10.1787/9789264204256-en.

Pearson (2017), *Pearson Edexcel Functional Skills qualification in Mathematics at Level 1 (FSM01) and Level 2 (FSM02)*, https://qualifications.pearson.com/content/dam/pdf/Functional-skills/Mathematics/2010/Specification-and-sample-assessments/Functional-Skills-Maths-Level-1-2.pdf.

Powell, A. (2017), *Apprenticeships Policy in England: 2017. House of Commons Briefing Paper 29 June 2017.*

Pullen, C. and J. Dromey (2016), *Earning and Learning: Making the Apprenticeship System Work for 16-18 year olds*, IPPR, www.ippr.org/files/publications/pdf/earning and-learning_Nov2016.pdf?noredirect=1.

Shildrick T. et al. (2012), *Poverty and Insecurity: Life in Low-pay, No-pay Britain*, The Policy Press.

Skills Funding Agency (2017), *Apprenticeship Grant: Employer Fact Sheet*, www.gov.uk/government/publications/apprenticeship-grant-employer-fact-sheet.

UK Commission for Employment and Skills (2016), *Employer Skills Survey 2015: UK Results. Evidence Report 97*, www.gov.uk/government/uploads/system/uploads/attachment_data/file/525444/UKCESS_2015_Report_for_web__May_.pdf.

Wiesman, J., P. Roe, and E. Parry (2013), "Evaluation of the apprenticeship grant for employers (age 16 to 24) programme", *BIS Research Paper,* No.157, http://dera.ioe.ac.uk/18949/1/bis-13-1318-evaluation-of-the-apprenticeship-grant-for-employers-age-16-to-24-programme.pdf.

Wolter, S. and P. Ryan (2011), *Apprenticeship. Handbook of Economics of Education*, Vol. 3, Elsevier North-Holland.

Young Women's Trust (2017), *Young Women and Apprenticeships: Still Not Working?*, Young Women's Trust, London, United Kingdom, www.youngwomenstrust.org/assets/0000/8200/Young_Women_and_apprenticeships.pdf.

Chapter 3. Developing work-based learning in England

This chapter looks at training delivered by and through the employer, and therefore primarily in the workplace. In England, training in the workplace is not systematic and subject to little quality assurance. In many apprenticeship systems training provided by employers in the workplace goes beyond training provided as part of the off-the-job training in England. The strategic objective should be to re-establish work-based training as a quality-assured and central attribute of English apprenticeships. Since work-based learning is the most effective way of preparing apprentices for working life, employers should be encouraged to take more responsibility for training in work places. This can be achieved by introducing regulations and standards for work-based learning, and by investing in the training capacity of employers.

Introduction: Key elements of apprenticeships

Work-based learning has been a defining feature of apprenticeships for millennia

This chapter is about work-based learning and work-based training in apprenticeship, meaning the learning and training delivered by and through the employer, and therefore primarily at work and in the workplace. In most countries and over most of recorded history, employer-provided work-based learning and training has been central to our understanding of apprenticeship. As far back as Babylonian times, apprenticeship has involved a contractual relationship between an employer-master-teacher and a worker-trainee, with the employer-master-teacher having the obligation to provide training, and the worker-trainee having the obligation to work (see Kedar, n.d.). This is reflected, for example, in the Oxford English Dictionary definition of an apprentice as "one who is bound by legal agreement to serve an employer in the exercise of some handicraft, art, trade, or profession, for a certain number of years, with a view to learn its details and duties, in which the employer is reciprocally bound to instruct him" (Oxford English Dictionary, 1979). Today, the same principle is found, for example in modern German apprenticeships, where all employers taking apprentices are described as 'training employers', since taking on an apprentice involves meeting a set of requirements to offer training (see, for example EU, 2017). Similarly in Norway employers offering apprenticeships have to be approved as 'training organisations'.

Work-based learning is a vital element in high-quality apprenticeships.

The workplace is a powerful learning environment, allowing hard skills to be learnt on the latest equipment, under the guidance and supervision of the practitioners who know how to use the equipment, while soft skills like teamwork and negotiation are acquired in context following the example of experienced professionals with these skills. It is no accident that this central defining feature of apprenticeship has allowed apprenticeship to maintain its status over millennia. External training providers inevitably find it difficult to keep up to date with technological and other change in the workplace, and teaching occupational skills in school workshops is often expensive because of the high cost of equipment. A Danish study (Westergaard and Rasmussen, 1999) compared the cost of apprenticeships, including subsidies to employers for provision of the on-the-job training, with the cost of apprenticeships provided entirely in schools. In the school-based apprenticeship, apprentices were receiving training, they would otherwise have received with employers, in school workshops. The study found the cost of the school-based apprenticeship was five times higher than the cost of apprenticeship with a work placement, even with the subsidy included. (see Kuczera, 2016 for more information on the benefits of work-based learning).

Policy issue 3.1: Developing work-based learning

Challenge: apprenticeship regulation does not currently provide adequate support for work-based development

In England, third-party training has supplanted work-based learning requirements

As apprenticeship has evolved historically in different countries, the longstanding obligation on an employer to provide instruction, was augmented by training and education provided by schools, colleges and other third-party training providers, forms of learning which provide a key complement to work-based learning. In most countries this additional element did not supplant the obligation on employers to provide training, and these employers were still required to provide effective training and an effective learning environment in the workplace. Many examples of these requirements on employers are given later in this chapter. In England, unusually, such obligations on employers appear to have been almost wholly supplanted by the expectations which fall on third-party training providers, including employers who are registered training providers or declared subcontractors (see Box 1.2 for the definition of off-the-job training in England). Many of the strongest English apprenticeships continue to offer training by the teacher-practitioner-employer that is not part of the 'off-the-job' training, but training in the workplace is not systematic and lacking quality assurance. In many apprenticeship systems training provided by employers in the workplace goes beyond training provided as part of the 'off-the-job' training in England.

Regulation is directed towards off-the-job training eligible for funding

In England, the primary focus of regulation and quality assurance is funded training. Only 'off-the-job' training, provided by a registered training provider, is eligible for funding. Such off-the-job training "involves learning which is undertaken outside of the normal day-to-day working environment and leads towards the achievement of an apprenticeship. This can include training that is delivered at the apprentice's normal place of work but must not be delivered as part of their normal working duties (Skills Funding Agency, 2017)." English and Maths are funded separately. Some of this 'off-the-job' training, eligible for funding in England, might be work-based learning. Employers can register as training providers and train their own staff. Some of the 'off-the-job' training provided can be subcontracted to employers by training providers and delivered in the workplace. Many employers clearly do provide work-based learning to apprentices that is not part of the off-the-job element, even though it is not directly funded through the levy or, in the past, by the government. But these are all possibilities rather than obligations on employers. In England, regulation of employers providing apprenticeships is limited: apprenticeship must be offered in jobs, called 'genuine jobs', providing apprentices with the opportunity to gain the knowledge, skills and behaviours needed to achieve apprenticeship (see Skills Funding Agency, 2017 for the description of 'genuine job'). But this requirement bears simply on the job role. There are effectively no other regulations on employers in respect of any training that they deliver, unless, as described above, they are employer-providers or subcontractors.

This lack of focus on work-based learning is a weakness

This approach distances English apprenticeship from employer training obligations, a core characteristic of apprenticeships that was visible in English apprenticeships for many centuries, that is even visible in the dictionary definition of apprenticeship, and remains visible in the apprenticeship systems of many other countries. Since work-based learning is highly desirable, this is a major challenge.

There would be real implementation challenges in requiring work-based learning

It is recognised that, if accepted as a goal, the development of work-based learning raises many challenges of implementation. First, employers, newly burdened with the levy, may not take kindly to additional obligations. Second, much policy attention is being given to ensuring the quality of the 'off-the-job training. This is understandable as in the past securing adequate off-the-job training in apprenticeships was a challenge. (Fuller and Unwin, 2008) report that many apprenticeships did not lead to the development of new skills and, in 2015 around one in five apprentices did not receive formal training, either within the workplace or at an external provider (Department for Education, 2016).

But the strategic objective should be to re-establish work-based training as a key characteristic of apprenticeships

These tactical obstacles, real as they are, should not stand in the way of a key strategic objective, of re-establishing employer-delivered work-based training as a central characteristic of English apprenticeship, an achievement which will be a necessary condition of England realising world class apprenticeships. This issue also goes to the broader ambitions embodied in the introduction of the apprenticeship levy, apprenticeship reform, and the target of three million starts. Since, as discussed at various points in this report, these ambitions will involve a substantial element of restructuring of other forms of human capital development into apprenticeship, this will only represent an achievement if the apprenticeships realised can demonstrate the highest quality. Moreover, as explained in this chapter, in the absence of more regulation of the employer role, there is a real risk that a significant proportion of apprenticeships will involve the exploitation of apprentices as unskilled labour.

Policy pointer 3.1: Developing work-based learning

As an integrated combination of external education and training and work-based learning is the most effective way of preparing apprentices for working life, employers should be encouraged to take more responsibility for work-based learning.

This can be achieved by introducing regulations and standards for work-based learning, and by investing in the training capacity of employers.

This may involve:

- Clarifying and strengthening, within the apprenticeship standards, what is expected of employers (as opposed to what is expected of training providers) in terms of work-based development that goes beyond the funded off-the-job training element. Work-based training should not only be fundable in principle, but encouraged or mandated systematically in all apprenticeships.
- Developing training for employer based supervisors of apprentices as part of a broader process of upgrading and professionalising work-based learning.
- Enhancing collaboration between training providers and employers, with training providers not only providing guidance to students in the workplace, but also providing guidance to workplace supervisors of apprentices over how practices at work can assist learning, and how productive work, linked to structured feedback on performance, can blend work and learning.
- Through active enforcement of standards on employers, ensuring that apprenticeship is not used to exploit apprentices as unskilled labour.
- Enforcing rigorously the existing minimum wage requirements for apprentices.

Analysis: Standards for work-based learning

Standards define the training responsibilities of employers

'Work-based learning standards' are regulations defining the competencies that should be developed in apprentices by employers through work-based learning, and other supporting regulations bearing on how that work-based learning should be delivered, such as those requiring relevant qualifications of apprentice supervisors. This type of apprenticeship regulation can be found in German speaking countries, in the Netherlands, Denmark and Norway Canada and Australia. For example, in Switzerland, there are requirements in terms of qualifications and training of apprentices' instructors in the employer, and how and where specific skills should be developed (see *plan de formation* at Confédération Suisse, 2018). In the Netherlands, a company offering apprenticeships must be accredited. The accreditation criteria require that supervisors working with apprentices are appropriately trained and qualified; the company offers sufficient training opportunities allowing apprentices to develop skills and competencies as defined in the curriculum; the company collaborates with the school providing off-the-job education and training, and the work environment is safe for apprentices (ECBO, 2016: 15-16). In Canada, employers are required to identify a certified journeyperson to supervise the apprentice (Canadian Apprenticeship Forum, 2017). Sometimes regulations are looser. In Australia apprentices are regular employees and the challenge is to ensure that apprentices receive training in addition to tasks performed within the framework of their regular job. Some Australian states tackle this issue by requiring people supervising apprentices to be qualified for this task. Training in the work place is also to some extent supervised and overviewed by the Registered Training Organisation (equivalent of registered training providers in England) (Queensland Government, 2018).

A diversity of approaches support the work-based learning capacity of employers

Some employers may not feel able to train apprentices, and some are better than others at conducting training on the job (see for example Kis, 2016). Training capacity depends on the quality of trainers, training methods and training equipment, and is typically less well developed in small companies that do not have dedicated training arrangements. Small companies may therefore particularly benefit from measures designed to enhance training capacity, such as training for trainers. Governments can enhance the training capacity of firms through a wide range of tools that include the provision of training for apprentice instructors; offering support materials to firms to help them develop their training skills; and facilitating networking among employers to share knowledge and experience on how best to support, develop and make use of apprentices. For example, Switzerland, in addition to formal requirements, provides in the QualiCarte a checklist of 28 quality criteria that are used by companies for self-assessment (OECD, 2010). Within the English context, a recent guide prepared by the Chartered Institute of Personnel and Development (CIPD) offers a range of advice to employers on best practice in mentoring and developing apprentices – but it is almost entirely voluntary (CIPD, 2017).

Analysis: Requirements for employees mentoring apprentices are an important element of work-based learning regulations

New apprentices need support in the workplace

Those who supervise and guide apprentices in their workplaces have heavy responsibilities, especially when apprentices are young. New apprentices not only have to learn a range of formal skills, but also need to acquire a diverse set of soft skills, in terms of how they work with colleagues, relate to their boss, communicate with customers and sometimes handle conflict. Young apprentices are also learning how to deal with life in the workplace, and may also, as teenagers transitioning to adulthood, have to tackle personal problems that may include issues like drug and alcohol abuse. In Switzerland, the full range of these issues is covered by the mandatory training courses for apprentice supervisors (see Box 3.1). Any one of these issues, if not well handled, could lead to the apprentice dropping out. Young apprentices from disadvantaged or troubled backgrounds, as discussed in Chapter 6, may face particular challenges. While, in England, employers taking young apprentices receive an extra thousand pounds and are exempted from National Insurance partly in recognition of these issues, there are no formal obligations in return.

In England, workplace support for apprentices is vital

In England there are no requirements for apprentices' instructors. But in practice this role, of guiding and supporting apprentices is a well-recognised and very important part of the strongest English apprenticeships, as emphasised by several apprentices and employers in evidence given to the parliamentary select committee (House of Commons, 2017). This led the select committee to recommend that, given growing numbers of apprenticeships, employers taking them on should "all have the knowledge and capacity to support and mentor these apprentices in the workplace". This recommendation is endorsed, and it should be implemented in practice through the development of regulatory standards.

In other countries, those guiding apprentices are often trained, and such training is sometimes mandatory

Box 3.1 describes requirements for employees who supervise apprentices; sometimes pedagogical training for these supervisors – it is compulsory in Germany and Switzerland, and in some trades in Ontario Canada and optional in Norway. Supervisors of apprentices may also be required to have an appropriate qualification and/or extensive work experience in the relevant occupation. Evidence suggests that better prepared apprentice supervisors reduce dropout. In Germany, the temporary suspension of compulsory training for apprentice supervisors was associated with higher apprentice dropout rates and more complaints on behalf of companies about the performance of apprentices. In the light of this experience, mandatory training for apprentice supervisors was reintroduced in 2009 after a six-year suspension.

Box 3.1. Country examples of training for apprentice supervisors in the workplace

In Canada, those who supervise apprentices must be qualified journeypersons. In Ontario in some trades supervisors need to have an additional qualification to train apprentices. The supervisor is expected to teach the required skills to the apprentice, regularly review with the apprentice their learning progress, and sign off on the relevant skills as they are learnt. Similarly in British Columbia, employers are responsible for teaching "the apprentice the skills of the trade by providing supervision and honest feedback from a certified journeyperson in the work environment".

Source: Employment Ontario (2017), "Hire an apprentice", www.ontario.ca/page/hire-apprentice (accessed 1 August 2017); The Industry Training Authority (ITA) (2017), "Apprenticeship who's who", www.itabc.ca/about-apprentices/apprenticeship-who%E2%80%99s-who (accessed 1 August.2017).

In Germany, those who supervise apprentices (typically holders of an upper secondary qualification) have to pass the trainer aptitude exam, while those with an advanced VET qualification (e.g. master craftsperson) already fulfil the requirements, since master craftsperson programmes include this element (BIBB, 2009a).

In the trainer aptitude exam (Ausbildereignungsprüfung), candidates demonstrate their ability to assess educational needs, plan and prepare training, assist in the recruitment of apprentices, deliver training and prepare the apprentice to complete their training (BIBB, 2009a). To prepare for the exam, candidates typically attend "Training for trainer" courses (Ausbildung für Ausbilder). These preparatory courses are provided by the chambers of commerce and normally last for 115 hours (BIBB, 2009b). Average costs are EUR 180 for the exam and up to EUR 420 for the preparatory course. Candidates may be supported by their employers and can seek financial support from the State through schemes such as the training credit (Bildungsprämie) (TA Bildungszentrum, 2015).

Source: BIBB (2009a), *Ausbilder-Eignungsverordnung Vom 21 Januar 2009*, Bundesgesetzblatt Jahrgang 2009 Teil I Nr. 5, www.bibb.de/dokumente/pdf/ausbilder_eignungsverordnung.pdf; BIBB (2009b), "Empfehlungen des Hauptausschusses des Bundesinstituts für Berufsbildung zum Rahmenplan für die Ausbildung der Ausbilder und Ausbilderinnen", www.bibb.de/dokumente/pdf/HA135.pdf; TA Bildungszentrum (2015), "Ausbildungseignungsprüfung IHK (AEVO)", www.ta.de/ausbildereignungspruefung-ihk-aevo.html.

In Norway, optional training is offered to employees involved in supervising apprentices. Some counties provide the training themselves, others ask schools or training offices (which are owned by companies collectively) to ensure its provision. The courses are free to participants since counties provide the course, learning material, subsistence and travel expenses. However, the firm is responsible for the supervisor's pay during the course.

Typically, the duration of the training is two days (or four half days) per year. Often there is a time interval between each training session, so that supervisors may practice what they have learnt and prepare a report, which is then presented at the next session. National guidelines, developed in co-operation with VET teacher training institutions, are available on the Internet and can be adapted to local needs. The form of training typically includes role-play and practice. Supervisors learn to cover the curriculum, complete evaluation procedures and administrative forms, prepare a training plan for apprentices, and follow through the plan.

Source: Norwegian Directorate for Education and Training (2009), personal communication (22 January 2009).

In Switzerland, apprentice supervisors are required to complete a targeted training programme, in addition to having a vocational qualification and at least two years of relevant work experience. Cantons are in charge of training, either by offering courses themselves or by delegating them to accredited training providers. They also subsidise these courses, which are offered in two formats leading to different qualifications (40 hour course costing SFR 600 or 100 hour course costing SFR 2 300). The training courses cover information about the Swiss VET system, vocational pedagogy and how to handle potential problems that may arise with young people (e.g. drugs, alcohol).

Source: ABB (n.d.), "Lehraufsicht", Amt für Berufsbildung und Berufsberatung, Thurgau, Amt für Berufsbildung und Berufsberatung, www.abb.tg.ch/xml_63/internet/de/application/d10079/d9739/f9309.cfm (accessed 26 February 2016); SBFI (n.d.), "Berufsbildungsverantwortliche", Staatssekretariat für Bildung, Forschung und Innovation, www.sbfi.admin.ch/berufsbildung/ (accessed 26 February 2016).

Analysis: Work-based Learning as a means of preventing the exploitation of apprentices

Regulation is necessary to ensure that employers provide apprentices with real opportunities to learn skills

There is nothing wrong with employers benefitting from the work of apprentices if low wages are compensated by an employer contribution to their training. As shown in Chapter 2, in many countries apprentice wages are kept below the wage of an unskilled employee, but individuals accept this cost if apprenticeship develops skills and competences associated with better employment and career opportunities. Conversely, if the motivation of employers is to use apprentices as a source of cheap unskilled labour, then it is much less likely that they will provide the environment required to learn a skilled job. Regulations and standards for training apprentices in the workplace provide a guarantee to apprentices that their willingness to work for low wages is worthwhile. They need to ensure that apprentices have an opportunity to develop a wide range of skills with the employer providing apprenticeship, and that they receive instruction and carry out skilled, as well as unskilled work. Two questions arise for England. Do employers have incentives to use apprentices as unskilled labour? Does regulation prevent this outcome?

Do employers have incentives to use apprentices as unskilled workers?

Using apprentices solely as unskilled labour requires little investment from employers but yields benefits associated with the productive unskilled work carried out by the apprentice. This issue is common to apprenticeship countries. Simulations based on cost-benefit surveys show that a Swiss employer could increase their net benefits by an average of EUR 22 000 per apprentice over the period of an apprenticeship if the apprentices performed only unskilled tasks while in the work place (Wolter and Ryan, 2011 in Muehlemann, 2016). Employers do not take advantage of this possibility in practice because of regulation. In England, employers will have incentives to substitute apprentices for unskilled workers if the costs of an apprentice are less than those of employing an unskilled worker, which is the case, as shown in Box 3.2. For example, for levy-paying employers, an apprentice at any wage below GBP 6 or below 80% of the minimum national wage would cost less than employing a worker at the national minimum wage (GBP 7.50). Drawing on 2013 data, around one-third of apprentices were paid 80% of the national minimum wage or less (BIS, 2014). For this group, there is a risk that that employers may have taken them on simply as the cheapest available source of unskilled labour. This comparison does not take into account the fact that employers with apprentices below the age of 25 are exempted from the National Insurance contribution amounting to 12% of the earning between GBP 157-GBP 866 per week (GOV.UK, 2018). Some small employers may also receive additional payments for taking on apprentices for the first time.

Box 3.2. Cost of an apprentice as compared to the cost of an unskilled worker (assuming minimum wages in both cases)

It is assumed the apprentice is 18 and above and is enrolled in an apprenticeship lasting one year. The cost of apprenticeship includes the apprentices wage cost (GBP 3.5 per hour) adjusted for the fact that apprentices spend 20% of their time off-the-job while being paid (www.gov.uk/national-minimum-wage-rates). Non-levy-paying employers' contribution of 10% of the programme cost is estimated as 10% of the average cost, (see funding bands at www.gov.uk/government/publications/apprenticeship-funding-bands).

Weekly (40 working hours) cost of an apprentice in a one year programme to an employer	Weekly (40 working hours) cost of an unskilled worker receiving the national minimum wage for their age
Levied employers: GBP 175 Non-levied employers: GBP 202 (GBP 175 + 10% of the cost of the programme)	Aged 25 and over: GPB 300 Aged 21-24: GBP 282 Aged 18-20:GBP 224

Note: An apprentice in the first year of apprenticeship has a minimum wage of GBP 3.50, as compared to the GBP 7.50 minimum wage generally applicable. It is assumed there are 40 working hours in a week.
Source: Adapted from GOV.UK (n.d.), "National minimum wage and national living wage rates", www.gov.uk/national-minimum-wage-rates, (accessed, 7 March 2017); GOV.UK (2018), "Apprenticeship funding bands", published 25 October 2016, (accessed 7 March 2017).

Regulation of apprentice jobs in England may not be sufficient to prevent exploitation

In principle, the use of apprentices as cheap labour might be prevented by the rule, mentioned earlier, that the apprentice "must have a job role (or roles) within the organisation that provides the opportunity for them to gain the knowledge, skills and behaviours needed to achieve their apprenticeship" (SFA, 2017). But enforcing this rule will be hard. Most job roles involve a mix of skilled and unskilled tasks, and learning opportunities require a reasonable proportion of apprentice time devoted to the skilled tasks. A job description might therefore meet the ESFA requirement in principle, but fail it in practice because inadequate apprentice time is spent in training and on skilled tasks. Some apprenticeship systems require employers of apprentices to log workplace activities – for example Canada requires employers to keep logs of on-the-job training and the type of work undertaken by apprentices (Canadian Apprenticeship Forum, 2017). More broadly, when most quality assurance is directed at the training provider, as in England, rather than employers in respect of their responsibilities (as in many other countries) enforcing this type of rule is bound to be difficult. In other countries requirements on the employers of apprentices cover not only the job role, but also their whole experience on the job, and the responsibilities of the employer to deliver work place development.

With the introduction of the apprenticeship levy the ESFA published new funding rules for employers, employer-providers, and training providers. These rules provide some additional quality control mechanisms by, for example defining the 20% off-the-job training requirement and clarifying employer and training provider obligations. However, it is clear that the majority of quality assurance and reporting measures continue to be directed at the training provider. The situation in England would be improved if (a) the commitment statement were strengthened by setting out the employers obligations for developing the apprentices while in work; and (b) through a more robust regime for monitoring training delivery.

Nearly one in five apprentices are paid less than the legally required apprentice minimum wage

The most recent apprentice survey found that nearly one in five (18%) of apprentices (Level 2 and 3) are paid wages below the legally required minimum. Among those aged 16-18 or in the first year of apprenticeship 13% were paid below the legal minimum (the minimum hourly apprentice wage for this group in 2016 was GBP 3.40 as compared to GBP 7.20 for those aged 25 and over). But among those aged 19 and over and in the second year of apprenticeship around one-third were paid below the legal minimum (BEIS, 2017). Among hairdressing apprentices about half receive wages below the legal minimum. Enforcement of minimum wages, according to the government official responsible, has been 'patchy' (Guardian, 2017). This is a serious problem, because it is widespread, it amounts to unlawful exploitation and this type of exploitation tends to stigmatise the whole apprentice brand.

A regulatory requirement for work-based learning would reduce the risk of exploitation

In conclusion, there is reason to suppose that the regulatory structure of apprenticeship leaves apprentices open to exploitation as cheap unskilled labour, and the large number of apprentices already being paid below the legal minimum reinforces this concern. The answer should be to make clear, enforceable demands on employers of apprentices to provide work-based training in a job role that supports such training. This requires a new approach to regulation, over and above the traditional regulation of funded training delivered by a registered provider.

References

BIS (2014a), "Apprenticeship pay survey 2014 ", *BIS Research Paper*, No. 207, www.gov.uk/government/publications/apprenticeship-pay-survey-2014.

BIS (2014b), "Apprenticeships evaluation: Learner survey 2014" , *BIS Research Paper*, No. 205, www.gov.uk/government/publications/apprenticeships-evaluation-learner-survey-2014.

Department of Business, Energy and Industrial Strategy (BEIS) (2017), "Apprenticeship pay survey 2016: England", *BEIS Research Paper*, No. 15, www.gov.uk/government/uploads/system/uploads/attachment_data/file/630082/apprenticeship-pay-survey-2016-report-england.pdf.

Canadian Apprenticeship Forum (2017), "Apprenticeship 101", http://caf-fca.org/apprenticeship-in-canada/apprenticeship-101/ (accessed 12 October 2017).

CIPD (Chartered Institute of Personnel and Development) (2017), *Apprenticeships that Work: A Guide for Employers*, www.cipd.co.uk/knowledge/fundamentals/people/routes-work/apprenticeships-guide.

Confédération Suisse (2018), " SBFI Berufsverzeichnis", www.becc.admin.ch/becc/public/bvz.

DfE (Department for Education) (2017), "Apprenticeship funding: How it Works", www.gov.uk/government/publications/apprenticeship-levy-how-it-will-work/apprenticeship-levy-how-it-will-work.

De Rick, K. (2008), "Costs and benefits of apprenticeships in the lowest track of VET", Schlögl (eds.), *Situated Competence Development through Innovative Apprenticeships. The Role of Different Stakeholders. Conference Proceedings International Network on Innovative Apprenticeship*, Österreichisches Institut für Berufsbildungsforschung, Vienna.

European Commission (2017), *Apprenticeship Toolbox: In-Company Training in Germany*, European Commission, www.apprenticeship-toolbox.eu/training-teaching/in-company-training/115-in-company-training-in-germany.

Fuller, A., and L. Unwin (2008), *Towards Expansive Apprenticeships. A Commentary by the Teaching and Learning Reserach Programme*, http://learning.gov.wales/docs/learningwales/publications/140721-towards-expansive-apprenticeships-en.pdf.

GOV.UK (2018), "National Insurance rates and categories", www.gov.uk/national-insurance-rates-letters.

Guardian (2017), "Bosses are failing to honour minimum pay laws, warns Britain's job market tsar", www.theguardian.com/society/2017/jul/29/minimum-wage-employers-abuses-david-metcalf (accessed 29 July 2017).

Hogarth, T., L. Gambin, and M. Winterbotham (2012), "Employer investment in apprenticeships and workplace learning: The fifth net benefits of training to employers study", *BIS research paper*, No. 67, www.gov.uk/government/publications/employer-investment-in-apprenticeships-and-workplace-learning-the-fifth-net-benefits-of-training-to-employers-study.

Jansen, A. et al. (2016), "Apprenticeship Training in Germany Remains Investment-Focused – Results of BIBB Cost-Benefit Survey 2012/13." BIBB Report 1/2015, www.bibb.de/en/25852.php.

Kedar, S. (n.d.), Apprenticeship in the Neo-Babylonian period: a study of bargaining power, www.biu.ac.il/js/Kramer/Aguda/Announc/Sivan%20Kedar%20-%20Apprenticeship%20in%20the%20Neo%20Babylonian%20Period%20+%20Table.pdf.

Kis V. (2016), "Work, train, win: Work-based learning design and management for productivity gains", *OECD Education Working Papers*, No. 135, OECD Publishing, Paris, http://dx.doi.org/10.1787/995fff01-en.

Kuczera M. (2017), "Striking the right balance: Costs and benefits of apprenticeship", *OECD Education Working Papers*, No. 153, OECD Publishing, Paris, http://dx.doi.org/10.1787/995fff01-en.

Muehlemann, S. (2016), "The cost and benefits of work-based learning", *OECD Education Working Papers*, No. 143, OECD Publishing, Paris. http://dx.doi.org/10.1787/5jlpl4s6g0zv-en.

OECD (2010), *Learning for Jobs*, OECD Publishing, Paris, http://dx.doi.org/10.1787/9789264087460-en.

Pfeifer, H. (2016), "Firms' Motivation for Training Apprentices: An Australian–German Comparison." NCVER, www.ncver.edu.au/publications/publications/all-publications/firms-motivation-for-training-apprentices-an-australian-german-comparison.

Poulsen, S. and C. Eberhardt (2016), *Approaching Apprenticeship Systems from a European Perspective, Bonn*, BIBB. http://pmb.cereq.fr/index.php?lvl=notice_display&id=58001.

Queensland Government (2018), The employer resources assessment and training plan – expectations of the department, https://training.qld.gov.au/apprenticeshipsinfo/information-resources/employer-capacity.

Richard, D. (2012), *The Richard Review of Apprenticeships,* School for Startups, London, United Kingdom, www.gov.uk/government/uploads/system/uploads/attachment_data/file/34708/richard-review-full.pdf.

Skills Funding Agency (2017), *Apprenticeship Funding: Rules for Employers May 2017 to March 2018*, www.gov.uk/government/uploads/system/uploads/attachment_data/file/612159/PROVIDER_V3__1_.pdf.

Strupler, M., S. Wolter, and M. Moser (2012), Die Duale Lehre: Eine Erfolgsgeschichte - Auch Für Die Betriebe : Ergebnisse Der Dritten Kosten-Nutzen-Erhebung Der Lehrlingsausbildung Aus Der Sicht Der Betriebe. Zürich: Rüegger.

ECBO (2016), "VET in the Netherlands." Cedefop, www.cedefop.europa.eu/files/4142_en.pdf.

Westergaard, N. and A. Rasmussen (1999), "The Impact of Subsidies on Apprenticeship Training." Centre for Labour Market and Social Research, Aarhus, http:/old-hha.asb.dk/nat/nwnart1.pdf.

Wolter, S. and P. Ryan (2011), *Apprenticeship. Handbook of Economics of Education*, Vol. 3, Elsevier, North-Holland.

Chapter 4. Funding of apprenticeship and the levy in England

This chapter compares the apprenticeship levy in England with other levy models around the world. It argues that the apprenticeship levy may have incentive effects, particularly on larger levy-paying employers, encouraging them to fund more apprenticeships. This raises two strategic challenges. The first is ensuring that the newly introduced apprentice standards, alongside other reforms, represent high quality, so that they fully deserve to be incentivised at the expense of other forms of training and skills development. The second linked challenge is to ensure that the funding rules, and other sources of public expenditure, provide effective funding for the apprenticeship system taken as a whole, so as to underpin the quality of individual apprenticeships.

Introduction: The apprenticeship levy in England

England shares with other countries some rationales for training levies

Levies on employers to pay for training – training levies – are found in more than 60 countries (OECD, 2017), while in the United Kingdom, sectoral training levies have existed for many years in the construction and engineering industries. In England, Wolf (2015), in an influential paper, argued that improvements in the quality and quantity of apprenticeships could not be realised without the much stronger funding that could be achieved through a training levy. One other factor driving the introduction of the levy was evidence of a decline in employer-provided training, suggesting that employers, if left to themselves, would not do enough to invest in workforce skills. Green et al. (2013), estimate that training hours halved between 1997 and 2011, while productivity growth remained low during the same period (Dolphin and Hatfield, 2015). The reasons for this decline in training are not entirely clear, and this evidence has been challenged (see Amin-Smith et al., 2017) but they may relate to casualization of employment, and an associated reduction in longer-term career entry positions that in the past would have attracted more substantial employer investment in training.

Larger employers pay into the levy

The levy is collected alongside national insurance at the rate of 0.5% of all payroll over GBP 3M – so that smaller employers with less than GBP 3M in payroll are exempted. While the requirement for employers to pay the levy is UK-wide, spending its proceeds involves devolved responsibilities, so the apprenticeship funding arrangements discussed here apply only to England.

These funds can then be accessed to pay for apprenticeships

Levy-paying employers are given a digital training account where they can see 'their' levy contributions accumulating in a fund topped up by a 10% contribution from the government. For apprentices in their workforce, employers may use this account to pay registered training providers to offer training, and (necessarily separate) registered assessment bodies to undertake end-point assessments. Funds entering the account must be used within 24 months. Employers who cannot call on these funds (either because they are small employers who pay nothing or little into the levy, or because they have exhausted the training account) must pay 10% of the training and assessment costs, with the government, through levy contributions, paying the remaining 90% (DfE, 2017).

Apprenticeships provided to young people attract higher funding

When a 16-18-year-old apprentice is taken on, both the employer and the training provider receive an additional GBP 1 000, and apprentices under 25 attract no national insurance contributions. Small businesses (with fewer than 50 employees) will also get 100% of the funding band for an apprentice aged 16-18 from the government rather than 90% as in the case of older apprentices for non-levy-paying employers as explained above. For employers who hire apprentices aged 19-24 who have previously been in care or who have a Local Authority Education, Health and Care plan, the government will pay for all the training costs and for apprentices with a learning or physical disability, the government will give an additional GBP 150 each month to cover extra learning costs (Powell, 2017).

How the apprenticeship levy in England compares with training levies around the world

The rationale for training levies

Training levies are used in many countries, with different rationales and target groups of trainees

There is a large concentration of training levies in Latin America and Africa, while sectoral levies for enterprise training (see Box 4.1) are common in Europe (see CEDEFOP, 2008; Whalley and Ziderman, 1990; Dar et al., 2003; Johanson, 2009; Ziderman, 2003). While occasionally training levies are used to fund apprenticeships, in most cases this is a relatively small part of their role. Levies are typically used to fund training for some combination of the existing workforce and new recruits. The policy rationale for levies varies between these groups.

- **For the existing workforce, market failures mean that employers tend to underprovide training.** While providing firm-specific skills, employers are more reluctant to train for the broader skills where, given the mobility of workers, workers themselves and other employers will be the main beneficiaries. Levy funding can correct this market failure, by supporting training that is in the collective interest of employers.
- **For the purposes of recruitment, employers benefit from a well-trained pool of potential recruits,** and should therefore contribute to the cost of the training through a levy (rather than, or in addition to, contributions from general taxation). This point may apply to the training of two potential groups:
  - Young labour market entrants receiving initial vocational education and training in schools and sometimes in apprenticeships. Some labour market levies, particularly in Latin America are primarily focused on this group, and have been used to support initial vocational training systems.
  - Adults in need of new skills, including the unemployed and those seeking career change. While the individuals concerned will benefit from the training, they can often not afford the full costs, and, on equity grounds, and in the collective economic interest, their training should be funded.

Sectoral levies

Levies limited to a single industrial sector are common, particularly in Europe. They are normally disbursement schemes, driven by employers in an industrial sector where employers see collective advantages from pooling training efforts. They can foster a close relationship between training and employer-defined skills needs in the sector, but such levies tend to be concentrated in sectors where employers are well organised and have a strong commitment to training (such as construction and engineering), so the capacity of sectoral arrangements to address skills weaknesses in other areas – for example retail and other service industries, is weaker. Sectoral funding may also neglect common core skills which are transferable across industries, and may be ill-adapted to regional needs (Ziderman, 2003; CEDEFOP, 2008).

Despite administrative challenges, levies should provide a stable pool of training resources

The collection of levies is an administrative burden on government, although it can be minimised by linking it to payroll taxes such as national insurance in the United Kingdom. There is an administrative burden on employers either seeking levy exemptions or funding for training, and if these are onerous some smaller employers may not seek funding (Dar et al. 2003; Johanson, 2009). But levies should provide a protected pool of training resources, with reserves to balance the pro-cyclical flow of income from the training levy (Johanson, 2009; Villalobos, Barria and Klasen, 2014).

Table 4.1. The dimensions of training levies

Governance	How funds are collected	How funds are spent
- initiative (public initiative based on national or local law / (inter)sectoral agreement between social partners / tripartite agreement / employer initiative), - coverage of levy scheme (universal / sectoral / regional) - funds management/governance (public sector, employer-led, bipartite, tripartite)	- source of funds (firm contributions only / government contribution) - collection method (social security agency / funds managing agency / tax administration) - type of levy (percentage of payroll / fixed amount per worker or working hour / percentage of profit /	- links to payments by levy-paying employers – as in levy exemption or other arrangements - recipients of funds (employer, training providers, training participants) - prioritised individuals (apprentices / unemployed / employees / disadvantaged groups) - location of training (within company / outside of company) - eligibility of training /approved training providers / recognised qualifications / approved programmes

Source: Adapted from Müller, N. and F. Behringer (2012), "Subsidies and levies as policy instruments to encourage employer-provided training", *OECD Education Working Papers*, No. 80, http://dx.doi.org/10.1787/5k97b083v1vb-en.

Disbursement and revenue-raising levies

Training levies are diverse in terms of governance, how funds are collected, and how they are spent (see Table 4.1). There are two main types – disbursement and revenue-raising.

Disbursement levies allow employers to call on levy funds to support their training efforts

Under disbursement schemes, employers are reimbursed from the fund for approved training (as in the new apprenticeship levy in England, and in, for example, the levy scheme in Malaysia). Some schemes allow employers to reduce their levy payment obligations by training ('train or pay', as in France). Disbursement levies are typically designed to increase employer *demand* for training. They offer a financial incentive for employers to train, while leaving them some control over what type of training to provide. The main disadvantage is the other side of the same coin - since employers decide when and where to train; the training provided might not always correspond to the broader needs of the economy (Johanson, 2009).

Revenue-raising levies aim to improve the supply of skills.

Revenue-raising levies (also referred to as 'traditional' or 'Latin American' schemes) are designed to increase the funding of training institutions, and in that way, increase the *supply* of skills. In contrast to disbursement schemes, they typically confer few or no rights on the levy-paying employer to access levy funds. Funds collected are used to support initial vocational training for young school leavers and labour market entrants to prepare them for jobs, and in-service training for the workforce (Dar, et al., 2003; Dougherty and Tan, 1991; Gasskov, 1994). Such schemes have played an important role in Latin America in developing vocational education and training systems. But they are sometimes associated with large bureaucracies, and the accumulation of unnecessary surpluses. It may be difficult to sustain employer interest, in the absence of direct incentives for enterprise training (Ziderman, 2003; CEDEFOP, 2008).

England uses a blend of approaches

While the levy in England is primarily a disbursement levy, since levy-paying employers can draw on levy funds to support training, it also has some elements of a 'revenue-raising' levy given the levy's role in funding initial apprenticeships for some part of the youth cohort. In fact, a blend of approaches is not uncommon in many countries (see Box 4.2). It is worth noting that the apprenticeship levy in England is not necessarily limited to the funding of apprenticeships by employers, but can be used for other purposes by the Department for Education.

Box 4.1. Singapore: A multipurpose training levy aligned with economic development

The Singapore Skills Development Fund (SDF), funded by a levy, provides financial incentives for training those in the workforce, as well as those joining the workforce. The Fund supports approved training plans through the Total Company Training Plan Scheme, and promotes special upskilling programmes such as the Training Assistance Scheme. It promotes a systematic approach to skills certification through a plan for training at least a third of a company's workforce in certifiable skills over a three-year period. The SDF also supports a training leave scheme for older workers and a special programme for IT training for SMEs.

A distinctive feature of the levy is that it is imposed only on the payroll for lower-wage workers earning SGD 4 500 (roughly EUR 3 000) or less a month. The current levy rate is 0.25% of monthly remuneration, or SGD 2, whichever is greater. Employers have a major role: 7 of the 15 members of the Singapore Workforce Development Authority (WDA), that controls the SDF, represent employers (including the Chairman and Vice-Chairman), with four for government and three for workers. Incentives for training are offered through cost-sharing, and the training must be relevant to the economic development of Singapore. The funding a company can obtain is not tied to the levy contribution. By 2013, WDA had trained over 1 million persons under the Workforce Skills Qualification (WSQ) system. The success of the system lies in the fact that skills and training were linked to economic development, and later on to foreign investment.

Source: OECD (forthcoming), "Training levies in Southeast Asia: What do they offer and how should they be organised? Lessons from global experience", *OECD Working papers*.

Implementing the apprenticeship levy: Messages from international experience

Taking account of the English context

There is a rationale for a training levy in England, but implementation challenges are multiple

In England, several factors, including skills gaps, barriers to school to work transition and high NEET (Not in Education, Employment or Training) rates, weak employer investment in training and poor productivity growth, argue for measures to enhance employer investment in skills. Levies represent an attractive means of addressing this challenge, given that they can support training both for school leavers and the existing workforce. But implementation presents many hurdles: under the wrong conditions, training levies can become bureaucratic, remote from employers, funding the training that would have taken place anyway. While systematic evidence from countries around the world is lacking, experience points to the major issues and challenges which need to be addressed when implementing levies. A recent OECD review (Kuczera, 2017) examines the broader evidence on financial incentives and apprenticeship.

How can training levies incentivise apprenticeship?

Both employer payments into the levy and levy funding of training have economic effects

Levies have two potential economic effects – depending on how they raise funds, and how these funds are spent. On the fund-raising side, a levy acts like a wage tax, but it can have distributional or incentive effects according to the fund-raising rules. For example, in Singapore, because the levy falls only on employers paying low wages, it may encourage an increase in wages to evade the levy, (and in skills to justify the higher wages), and/or it might, by increasing the cost of employing the low-skilled, raise their unemployment risk. If (as is often the case, including in the United Kingdom) smaller employers are exempt from a levy, the levy may help smaller employers if they also benefit from training levy expenditure.

Some important incentive effects are not strictly economic

Training levies are often intended to give employers a sense of ownership of, and involvement in training, as in England. This may be because employers see 'their' money being channelled into training, but it may also be because employers are directly involved in managing the training fund and identifying training priorities, or, at an individual employer level, because developing a training plan is sometimes necessary to receive funding. Rather few countries have levy systems specifically designed, as in the new levy in England, to support apprenticeships. Two countries that do have such systems, with some quite special characteristics that differentiate them from the levy in England, are Denmark and France (see Box 4.2).

Box 4.2. Employer levies to support apprenticeship in France and Denmark

France maintains a complex mix of incentives encouraging employers to offer apprenticeships. A training levy in the form of an apprenticeship tax is set at 0.5% of the wage bill, plus an additional 0.18% tax contribution to a separate 'apprenticeship development' fund, and, for businesses with 250 employees or more, a further contribution which varies with the percentage of their employees in work-based vocational training (apprenticeships and some other schemes). Most funds from these taxes are funnelled through intermediary bodies and the regions to offer employers a tax credit of EUR 1 600 per apprentice and an allowance of at least EUR 1 000 per apprentice. Employers are also largely exempt from social security contributions on their apprentices (a substantial benefit in France where such contributions are much higher than in the United Kingdom). Employers may also opt for some of their contributions to the apprentice tax to go directly to the local training institutions that they designate, including higher education institutions, independently of the apprenticeship training role of these institutions, although following recent reforms, only around 23% of the apprenticeship tax is now so allocated.

Denmark maintains a dual apprenticeship system supported by an employer levy system. All employers, public and private, contribute to the Employers' Reimbursement Fund a fixed amount for each employee (in 2016, around EUR 370 per year). Levy funds are used primarily to pay apprentice salaries while apprentices are pursuing off-the-job training.

Reimbursements may exceed the wage in some cases. There are bonuses for youth who find a paid apprenticeship without assistance. Apprentice wages are set at the sector level through collective agreements and typically reach 40 to 50% of the minimum wage. Apprenticeship programmes consist in a basic (academic) and a main (practical) programme. For the main programme, the student must find a training agreement with a company approved by the social partners. When undertaking the main programme, students alternate between training periods in the company and practical education at the college. Overall, 50 to 70% of practical education takes place in a company. Social partners are closely involved in the organisation of the system,

Source : Conseil d'Analyse Économique (2014), L'apprentissage au service de l'emploi Les notes du conseil d'analyse économique, no 19, December 2014, www.cae-eco.fr/IMG/pdf/cae-note019-env2.pdf; OECD (2014), *OECD Economic Surveys: Denmark 2013*, http://dx.doi.org/10.1787/eco_surveys-dnk-2013-en.

Funding from government and levies can support different aspects of apprenticeship

The funding of apprenticeships, by government or through a levy, can take different forms, including:

- *Direct financial contributions or tax breaks* for employers providing apprenticeships - the most common form of support. In Norway, the government provides companies a subsidy per apprentice of around EUR 14 800[1] per year of work placement. In Austria, employers receive a subsidy per apprentice in the first year that is equivalent to three gross apprentice wages, an equivalent of two gross apprentice wages in the 2nd year, and an equivalent of one gross apprentice wage in the 3rd and 4th year (Federal Ministry of Science, Research and Economy 2014). In France employers receive an allowance and a tax credit for each apprentice (see Box 4.2).
- *Paying for off-the-job training – as in the levy in England.* In nearly all countries with apprenticeship systems, including most apprenticeship systems in continental Europe, off-the-job training is funded through state funding of the vocational training providers. In that respect, the English apprenticeship levy is unusual. Although there is an economic argument that the levy is an employment tax, there are some important behavioural differences emerging. One of them is that large employers state that they intend to use their funds if they possible can. This means that they do not treat their levy payments as a sunk cost in the way they would treat a normal employment tax.
- *Paying wages to apprentices when they are pursuing off-the-job training.* In most countries, employers bear this cost directly, although it may be factored into the negotiated pay of apprentices, which is usually below the minimum wage. But this is the specific function of the employer's levy in Denmark (see Box 4.2), while in Ireland the government pays a training allowance to apprentices while they are being trained off the job. Implicitly these are (quite substantial) subsidies to employers providing apprenticeships.

Table 4.2. Financial incentives to companies providing apprenticeships

	Tax incentives*	Subsidy	Levy scheme
Australia	Tax incentives depend on the qualifications the programme leads to	Subsidy in specific cases e.g. person being trained has a disability	No
Austria	Tax incentives abolished in 2008 and replaced by targeted subsidies	From 2008, targeted subsidies have been available per apprentice (the amount depends on the year of apprenticeship), for additional training, for training of instructors, for apprentices excelling on final assessment, for measures supporting apprentices with learning difficulties, and equal access for women to apprenticeships	A levy fund in the construction sector covers all regions and a levy fund in the electro-metallic industry covers one province (Vorarlberg). Both negotiated by employers and Trade Unions
Belgium – Flanders	Payroll tax deduction	Direct subsidy depending on the number of apprentices and programme duration	No
Germany	No	No	In the construction sector. Negotiated by employers and trade unions
Netherlands	Tax exemptions (abolished in 2014)	From 2014, subsidy to employers up to EUR 2 700 per apprentice per year (depending on the duration of the apprenticeship)	No
Norway	No	Direct subsidy depending on the number of training places, equity role (e.g. to encourage enterprises to take up disadvantaged trainees), and sector	No
Switzerland	No	No	All companies within certain economic sectors can decide to contribute to a corresponding vocational fund (to develop training, organise courses and qualifications procedures, and promote specific occupations)

Note: Tax incentives include: (a) tax allowances (deducted from the gross income to arrive at the taxable income); (b) tax exemptions (some income is exempted from the tax base); (c) tax credits (sums deducted from the tax due); (d) tax relief (some classes of taxpayers or activities benefit from lower rates); (e) tax deferrals (postponement of tax payments).

Source: Adapted from Kuczera (2017), "Incentives for apprenticeship", *OECD Education Working Papers*, No. 152, http://dx.doi.org/10.1787/55bb556d-en.

Different subsidy arrangements in other countries may reflect different apprenticeship systems

So, in summary, countries offer a wide variety of subsidies for apprenticeships (see Table 4.2), only occasionally supported by levy arrangements. Often, they involve a direct transfer or subsidy to employers to encourage them to take on apprentices, perhaps recognising the role of employers in delivering training on the job.

How effective are apprenticeship subsidies: deadweight and displacement?

Most evidence suggests the direct effects of apprenticeship subsidies for employers are modest

Westergaard and Rasmussen (1999) report a modest positive effect of public subsidies on the offer of apprenticeship places in Danish firms, but only in manufacturing, office and retailing. In Austria, the subsidies appear to have had a limited impact (Wacker, 2007). In

Switzerland (where there are no subsidies of this type) a simulation exercise suggested that subsidies would have an impact on firms not currently involved in apprenticeships but no effect on the supply of apprenticeship training in firms that train already (Muehlemann, 2016). An evaluation of the Australian scheme shows that the subsidy had only a small impact on the decision of employers to train, mainly because the subsidy covered only a small part of the employer cost of offering an apprenticeship (Deloitte, 2012). One reason for the modest impact may be the 'deadweight' involved.

Apprenticeship subsidies often involve substantial deadweight

'Deadweight' is training that employers would have funded anyway, even in the absence of the relevant incentive. Deadweight can be most effectively minimised when the target group is homogeneous in terms of the cost-benefit balance, so that a given incentive can be calculated to be just sufficient to reach a tipping point, where it will push a large proportion of the target group to alter their behaviour, minimising deadweight. But the cost-benefit balance of apprenticeships may be heterogeneous – implying substantial deadweight. While in England the costs and benefits of apprenticeship to employers will be different because of different design features, a similar level of heterogeneity in net benefits is plausible, again implying a substantial amount of deadweight.

There is a tension between employer buy-in and the minimisation of deadweight

The aim of levy funding is to change behaviour. By definition, this is not what employers would do, if left to themselves. This means that there is always going to be some degree of tension between the minimisation of deadweight and employer buy-in. This tension may be managed most effectively if the training levy achieves what employers *collectively* want to see, recognising that employers may collectively want to have, and even pay for, a well-skilled labour force, even if, at individual employer level, they might not see a direct return from investing in their own workers.

Measures to reduce deadweight focus on additionality

Sometimes attempts are made to avoid deadweight by limiting subsidies to *additional* apprenticeships. In Austria there is a subsidy for employers providing 'new' apprenticeship places (Federal Ministry of Science, Research and Economy, 2014). A tax allowance for training introduced in Flanders was limited to companies that could show they were increasing overall training (Muller and Behringer, 2012). In England, a special payment of GBP 1 500 per apprentice is made available to smaller employers who have not recruited an apprentice in the last 12 months and want to take an apprentice aged 16-24 (Skills Funding Agency, 2017). But additionality tests can be hard to enforce, and may be seen as unfair if funding is denied to employers with a stable and longstanding commitment to apprenticeships, in favour of companies which qualify for funding simply because they are expanding and are therefore taking on more apprentices.

Well-structured incentives may improve the quality, as well as the quantity of training

Evaluation of incentive effects merely in terms of the quantity of deadweight can be simplistic. Often the effect of incentives and subsidies will be to reconfigure the mix of training, by substituting or displacing one form of training not eligible for subsidy with a related or similar form of training which is so eligible. This is sometimes distortionary: in the Netherlands, a 1998 tax law allowed firms to claim 120% of their training expenditure as a tax deduction for workers under 40, and 140% for those over 40, with the objective of encouraging training of older workers. But the effect was that training was redistributed from workers slightly below the age of 40 to those just over 40 (Leuven and Oosterbeek,

2004). But if, for example, funding incentives make quality assurance of training a requirement, the effect may be to substitute training of variable quality with good quality training. So, when measuring additionality, qualitative as well as quantitative additionality needs to be assessed – a point of key relevance to England.

The effects of the levy in England

No employer has to meet much of the cost of off-the-job training in apprenticeship

With the levy in place, no employer – levy-paying or not – ever has to contribute more than 10% of the direct cost of apprentice training should they choose to take an apprentice (over and above any mandatory levy payments, which do not directly affect the incentives to take apprentices). The only exceptions would be employers who choose an apprenticeship costing more than the standard funding bands. Although employers face other costs, including the opportunity cost of releasing apprentices for training at least 20% of their working time, this is balanced by other incentives such as no national insurance contributions for the under-25s, lower wages, plus direct financial incentives to employers when they take apprentices aged 16-18, and in some other cases. This means that employers will usually have incentives to use apprenticeship training as long as they can obtain modest returns to them, recognising the points made above, that financial incentives usually have limited impact, and deadweight is substantial.

The incentive effects of the levy create two challenges

The apprenticeship levy could have incentive effects, particularly on larger levy-paying employers, encouraging them to use the levy, particularly where it may be used to replace other forms of training and skills development. This raises two strategic challenges. The first is that of ensuring that the newly introduced apprentice standards, alongside other reforms, represent high quality, so that they fully deserve to be incentivised at the expense of other forms of training and skills development. The second linked challenge is to ensure that the funding rules, and other sources of public expenditure, provide effective funding for the apprenticeship system taken as a whole, so as to underpin the quality of individual apprenticeships. These challenges form the substance of discussion below, and provide a backdrop to the analysis of later chapters in this review.

The number of people starting apprenticeships dropped after the introduction of the apprenticeship levy

First evaluations show a drop in apprenticeship starts after introduction of the levy (GOV.UK, 2016). There is some evidence showing that employers do not understand the new system and find it difficult to navigate (Butler, 2018). More demanding requirements for apprenticeship may also deter some employers from providing it. This is not necessarily a bad thing if it removes from the market low quality apprenticeships. Recognising that the apprentice levy was only introduced in 2017, further evaluation is required to fully appreciate its impact on apprenticeship provision. Some of the encountered challenges such as the low level of understanding of the new apprenticeship by employers can be easily addressed by making the system more user-friendly.

Policy issue 4.1: Giving priority to quality

Challenge: The incentive effects of the apprenticeship levy

How positive these effects will be will depend on the quality of the apprenticeship system

The levy will reconfigure other forms of skills development as apprenticeships, a reconfiguration that will be desirable where loosely organised training is replaced by quality apprenticeships, delivering skills of relevance to the industry, not just to the individual employer. But in other contexts the substitution will be undesirable, where training that might be more efficiently handled on an *ad hoc* basis, is artificially restructured into an apprenticeship. In some cases, additional incentive effects will be important, in the case of degree apprenticeships (where avoiding student loans is a powerful driver) and in the public sector, given new targets. These cases are discussed in Chapter 7.

Policy pointer 4.1: Giving priority to quality

Evidence suggests that the introduction of the levy may have significant incentive effects on levy-paying employers, who will seek to increase apprentice numbers to spend their levy contributions. Often this will involve restructuring other training and replacing other means of recruiting skilled workers. To ensure that the levy incentives work constructively, the strongest possible quality assurance measures will be needed so that apprenticeship training is of high quality, so that the restructuring involved adds value.

Analysis: Quality as the most essential element of apprenticeship reform

This policy pointer is deliberately broad

It is designed to underpin the more detailed analysis of quality issues in the chapters which follow, including not only the specific points on quality in Chapter 5, but also all the other suggestions put forward in other chapters. Quality is always important, but at a time when England is seeking to increase the numbers of apprenticeships directly, and through incentives that will replace other means of skills development, quality becomes the priority of priorities. 'Adequate' apprenticeship quality is not good enough when it replaces another form of skills development which may also be adequate. Realising the target of 3 million apprenticeship starts by 2020 will be of no value unless they correspond to high-quality apprenticeships.

Policy issue 4.2: Funding for an effective apprenticeship system

Challenge: Levy funding is only currently available for limited parts of an effective apprenticeship system

Some parts of an effective apprenticeship system are not currently supported by the levy

An effective apprenticeship system, as illustrated in international experience, is a system with multiple vital elements, all of which demand resources. For young people, still teenagers, it will, as discussed in Chapter 2, include a broad education, equipping them as citizens, as well as for a career. As discussed in Chapter 3, it will include on-the-job training, delivered by experienced workplace practitioners, who have received professional training in how to train apprentices. It will, as discussed in Chapter 6, include support for apprentices who struggle to complete their programmes, and need independent advice and mentoring to do so, and guidance and support if they do drop out; it will also include effective pre-apprenticeship programmes, in diverse forms which prepare young people with limited skills and attainment for entry into demanding apprenticeship programmes. It will, as discussed in Chapter 7, include arrangements to support employers in seeing how to make best use of apprenticeships, and facilitate co-ordination that will allow smaller employers to work together locally to support apprenticeship. Most of these elements are already found in England in the strongest apprenticeships, but in at least some other countries, they are supported more systematically. The levy supports important but incomplete elements of an effective apprenticeship system – namely training delivered primarily by external training providers, and the associated assessments. While the levy is not appropriate for funding many other aspects of the apprenticeship system, such as general education, it may be explored whether public funds or action could support other elements of an effective apprenticeship such as stronger regulations setting out the employers obligations for developing the apprentices while in work.

The levy is designed to ensure that more training takes place

In the past, as noted in Richard (2012), and in many other contexts, some formally recognised, 'apprenticeships' were delivered with very little training, as they corresponded to certifications of existing skills, and this seriously damaged the apprenticeship brand. One argument for limiting the apprenticeship levy to the funding of clearly recognisable training, alongside assessments, is that it avoids the leakage of levy funds into a host of other activities of questionable desirability which employers or providers might like to pursue, all of which would be difficult to audit. This is a strong argument, but it needs to be balanced by recognition of the importance of the other elements of a quality apprenticeship system, set out above. These elements need to be supported in one way or another.

Policy pointer 4.2: Funding for an effective apprenticeship system

Under current rules, the apprenticeship levy provides funding for apprentice training and assessments delivered by registered training providers and assessment bodies, but not to other bodies or for other purposes. Quality assurance in the system primarily follows the funding, and therefore looks at these activities and bodies. However, an effective apprenticeship system involves a wide range of broader functions, including the development of the apprentice in the workplace by the employer (in parallel to any off-the-job training), the broader education of young apprentices, preparation for apprenticeship through traineeship and other pre-apprenticeship schemes, support and advice for apprentices and training employers seeking to get the best out of the apprenticeship system. While it may not be appropriate to fund these activities through the levy, they do need to be supported, funded where necessary and their quality assured.

Analysis: Supporting wider elements of an effective apprenticeship system

Support will be necessary for other parts of an effective apprenticeship system

One significant risk is that the effect of the levy will be to expand apprenticeships through a too exclusive focus on off-the-job training and assessments, but without an adequate complement and infrastructure in all the other elements of quality apprenticeship, which are not open to levy funding. Larger employers may, for example, use levy funding 'creatively' to replace some existing high-quality employer-delivered and employer-funded work-based training with an apprenticeship programme, largely delivered off the job by an external training provider, simply because of the availability of levy funding for this purpose. The risks that this may occur and its potential undesirability have been identified for example by OECD (2017). The wider issues involved in supporting work-based training delivered by employers are addressed in Chapter 3. Funds, and other support, could also be made available to support wider elements of an effective apprenticeship system, including the support for traineeships and pre-apprenticeship programmes, training of workplace trainers (perhaps through an apprenticeship programme), and by providing local support for individual apprentices at risk of dropout.

Note

[1] Based on currency NOR/EUR exchange rate, 5 April 2016.

References

Amin-Smith, N., J. Cribb and L. Sibieta (2017), *Reforms to apprenticeship funding in England* Institute for Fiscal Studies. www.ifs.org.uk/uploads/publications/budgets/gb2017/gb2017ch8.pdf.

Butler S. (2018), "Fall in apprenticeships May force 'radical rethink' of UK policy", *The Guardian,* Thursday 25 January 2018, www.theguardian.com/education/2018/jan/25/fall-in-uk-apprenticeships-may-force-radical-rethink-of-policy,(accessed 27 February 2018).

BPP University (2017), *Employer Guide: Apprenticeship Levy Study.* http://employers.bpp.com/assets/guides/The_Apprenticeship_Levy_Study.pdf.

CEDEFOP (2008), "Sectoral training funds in Europe", *European Centre for the Development of Vocational Training Panorama Series,* No.156. Luxembourg.

Conseil d'Analyse Économique (2014), *L'apprentissage au service de l'emploi* Les notes du conseil d'analyse économique, No 19, December 2014, www.cae-eco.fr/IMG/pdf/cae-note019-env2.pdf.

Dar, A. and T. Whitehead (2003), *Training Levies: Evidence from Evaluations*, World Bank Employment Policy Primer No. 6. World Bank. Washington, DC, http://documents.worldbank.org/curated/en/2003/12/8913510/training-levies-evidence-evaluations.

Deloitte (2012), *Econometric Analysis of the Australian Apprenticeships Incentives Program*, Deloitte Access Economics, Kingston Australia, www.australianapprenticeships.gov.au/sites/ausapps/files/publicationdocuments/econometricanalysisaaip.pdf.

DfE (Department for Education) (2017), *Apprenticeship Funding: How it Will Work,* www.gov.uk/government/publications/apprenticeship-levy-how-it-will-work/apprenticeship-levy-how-it-will-work.

Dolphin T. and I. Hatfield (2015), *The Missing Pieces: Solving Britain's Productivity Puzzle*, IPPR, www.ippr.org/publications/the-missing-pieces-solving-the-uks-productivity-puzzle.

Dougherty, C. and J.P. Tan (1991), "Financing training: Issues and options", *The World Bank Working Paper Series,* No. 716, Washington, DC.

Federal Ministry of Science, Research and Economy (2014), *Apprenticeship: Dual Vocational Education and Training in Austria Modern Training with a Future,* www.bmwfw.gv.at/Berufsausbildung/LehrlingsUndBerufsausbildung/Documents/Die_Lehre_HP_engl.pdf.

Gambin, L.et .al. (2016), *The Apprenticeship Levy: How will employers respond?*, Department for Education Research report, www.gov.uk/government/uploads/system/uploads/attachment_data/file/562445/The_apprenticeship_levy_how_will_employers_respond.pdf.

Gasskov, V. (ed.). (1994), *Alternative Schemes of Financing Training*, Geneva: International Labour Office.

GOV.UK (2016), "Collection. statistics: Further education and skills", Further education and skills data reported for January 2014 to present", www.gov.uk/government/collections/further-education-and-skills-statistical-first-release-sfr#2017-releases.

Green, F.et al. (2013), *What Has Been Happening to the Training of British Workers?,* Centre for Learning and Life Chances in Knowledge Economies and Societies, http://www.llakes.org.

Johanson, R. (2009), "A review of national training funds", *SP Discussion Paper*, No. 0922, The World Bank, Washington, DC.

Kuczera, M. (2017), "Incentives for apprenticeship", *OECD Education Working Papers*, No. 152, OECD Publishing, Paris. http://dx.doi.org/10.1787/55bb556d-en.

Leuven, E. and H. Oosterbeek (2004), "Evaluating the effect of tax deductions on training", *Journal of Labor Economics,* Vol. 22/2, www.economists.nl/files/20070903-leuvenOosterbeek2004jole.pdf.

Müller, N. and F. Behringer (2012), "Subsidies and levies as policy instruments to encourage employer-provided training", *OECD Education Working Papers*, No. 80, OECD Publishing, Paris, http://dx.doi.org/10.1787/5k97b083v1vb-en.

OECD (forthcoming), "Training levies in Southeast Asia: What do they offer and how should they be organised? Lessons from global experience", *OECD Working papers*.

OECD (2017), *Getting Skills Right: United Kingdom*, OECD Publishing, Paris, http://dx.doi.org/10.1787/9789264280489-en.

Powell, A. (2017), *Apprenticeships Policy in England: 2017 House of Commons Briefing Paper 29 June 2017*.

Richard, D. (2012), *The Richard Review of Apprenticeships,* School for Startups, London, United Kingdom, www.gov.uk/government/uploads/system/uploads/attachment_data/file/34708/richard-review-full.pdf.

Skills Funding Agency (2017), *Apprenticeship Grant: Employer Fact Sheet,* www.gov.uk/government/publications/apprenticeship-grant-employer-fact-sheet.

Villalobos Barría, C. and S. Klasen (2014), "The impact of SENAI's vocational training programme on employment, wages, and mobility in Brazil: What lessons for Sub-Saharan Africa?", *International Research Initiative on Brazil and Africa* (IRIBA), *Working Paper,* No.05, University of Manchester, Manchester, United Kingdom.

Wacker, K. (2007), "Teure Neue Lehrstelle. Eine Untersuchung Zur Effizienz Des Blum- Bonus", NÖ Arbeiterkammer, Vienna.

Westergaard, N. and A. Rasmussen (1999), *The Impact of Subsidies on Apprenticeship Training*, Centre for Labour Market and Social Research, Aarhus, Denmark, www.researchgate.net/publication/265272135_The_impact_of_subsidies_on_Apprenticeship_Training.

Whalley, J. and A. Ziderman (1990), "Financing training in developing countries: The role of payroll taxes", *Economics of Education Review*, Vol. 9/4, pp. 377-87.

Wolf, A. (2015), *Fixing a Broken Training System: The Case for an Apprenticeship Levy,* Social Market Foundation, July 2015, www.smf.co.uk/wp-content/uploads/2015/07/Social-Market-Foundation-Publication-Alison-Wolf-Fixing-A-Broken-Training-System-The-Case-For-An-Apprenticeship-Levy.pdf.

Ziderman, A. (2003), "Financing vocational training to meet policy objectives: Sub-Saharan Africa", *African Region Human Development Series*, The World Bank, Washington, DC.

Chapter 5. Quality in apprenticeship qualifications and assessment in England

Quality assurance faces new requirements given the introduction of the apprenticeship levy, the replacement of frameworks by standards and other connected reforms. This chapter argues that apprentice standards need to be coherent with the wider system of vocational qualifications and manageable in number. They should be designed so as to ensure the transferability of skills and allow for the recognition of prior learning. England proposes to achieve consistency in assessment standards through multiple bodies conducting the assessment. The chapter argues that given the key role of consistent assessment standards in the credibility and reputation of apprentice qualifications these plans should be reviewed.

Introduction: The role of quality

Quality in apprenticeship policy in England and around the world

The shift from frameworks to standards is intended to enhance quality

In England, plans to expand the number of apprenticeships have been matched by reforms which aim to improve quality, through a new form of apprenticeship embodied in apprenticeship 'standards', and new quality assurance institutions. These reforms are taking place against a background of concern that, previously, too many apprenticeships were undemanding and low level, and were therefore not providing the substantial contribution to workforce skills that might be needed by the economy, or expected of the apprenticeship brand. Chapter 4 argued that quality should be the priority of apprenticeship reform because the levy is likely to encourage the restructuring of other forms of skills development as apprenticeship.

'Quality' as an explicit goal, emerged first in management theories

The notion of quality has in recent decades become more prominent in public policy debate, including in relation to vocational education and training (see for example European Training Foundation, 2014). The language used can be fluid, so that quality 'management', quality 'control', quality 'improvement' and quality 'assurance' are all used somewhat interchangeably, but also to impart different nuances. In the context of vocational education and training, concerns about low quality led to the establishment of the European Quality Assurance Reference Framework for Vocational Education and Training (EU, 2009).

At its widest, good 'quality' means anything desirable

Quality potentially covers all desirable features of apprenticeship. Quality may be attributed to the highest 'system' level covering the entire apprenticeship system, at a more intermediate 'design' level, covering individual apprenticeship programmes and qualifications, and at the 'delivery level, covering the learning experience of the individual apprentice. Thus a strong apprenticeship system will support the design of individual apprentice qualifications – for example through a qualifications framework that provides clarity about the relationship between apprenticeship and wider educational qualifications. Good design, in the form of the right qualification will then underpin effective delivery of individual apprenticeships. Quality and quality assurance in vocational education and training are commonly associated with some combination of inputs, processes and outputs (EU, 2009; European Training Foundation, 2014; Broek and Buiskool, 2013; Sweet, 2014). These may be taken to apply at the system, design or delivery stage, implying a matrix as in Table 5.1.

Table 5.1. Types of quality and quality assurance in apprenticeship and the levels at which they may be applied

	Inputs	Processes	Outputs
System features such as wide coverage across different industrial sectors, high status and a good brand, extensive employer buy-in. Strong and effective support institutions in terms of a legal and institutional framework that engages key actors in supporting the system.	e.g. Strong policy-making bodies, co-ordinating institutions	e. g. Effective consultation procedures	e. g. Well-respected apprenticeship system
Design features such as well constructed qualifications, apprentice standards and approaches to assessment relevant to labour market needs. Apprentice wages that work for both apprentice and employer.	e. g. Well-qualified people, preparing qualifications and standards, adequate input from employers	e. g. Time and resources to construct qualifications, standards etc. Arrangements for updating.	e.g. Well-respected qualifications and standards, meeting employer and student needs
Delivery, especially training quality and effectiveness.	e. g. Accredited training providers, well-trained trainers	e. g. Pedagogical technique	e. g. High completion rates and good labour market outcomes

Source: Adapted from Broek, S. and B.-J. Buiskool (2013), *Developing the Adult Learning Sector: Quality in the Adult Learning Sector (Lot 1), Final Report (Open Call for tender EAC/26/2011)*, Panteia, Zoetermeer, http://arhiv.acs.si/porocila/Quality_in_the_Adult_Learning_Sector-final_report.pdf; Ulicna, D. and A. Curth (2013), *Study on quality assurance in continuous VET and on future development of EQAVET, Final Report*, ICF GHK, Brussels, www.eqavet.eu/Libraries/2014_Publications/Study_on_QA_in_CVET.sflb.ashx; Sweet, R. (2014), *Work-based Learning: A Handbook for Policy Makers and Social Partners in ETF Partner Countries, prepared for the ETF (European Training Foundation)*, http://ec.europa.eu/education/library/publications/etf-wbl-handbook_en.pdf; European Training Foundation (2014), *Quality assurance in vocational education and training a collection of articles*, European Training Foundation; EU (2009). *Recommendation of the European Parliament and of the Council of 18 June 2009 on the Establishment of a European Quality Assurance Reference Framework for Vocational Education and Training*, http://eur-lex.europa.eu/legal-content/EN/TXT/PDF/?uri=CELEX:32009H0708(01)&from=EN.

Reform and a new approach to quality in England

Some serious quality problems were identified in the past

Under the apprenticeship frameworks – now being phased out in England - serious quality weaknesses in some sectors have coexisted with strands of high-quality provision. Ofsted used a survey of providers, apprentices and employers to show that in around one-third of the providers, apprentices were not receiving sufficient high-quality training, and were often just having their existing low-level skills accredited; this was particularly likely among apprentices aged over 25, especially at employer-providers in the retail and care sectors. Often providers lacked a clear rationale for their apprenticeship programmes in terms of local labour market requirements. Conversely, the report noted the high quality of many apprenticeships in some more technical areas (Ofsted, 2015). The regular apprenticeship evaluation exercise (BIS, 2014) also revealed that a significant minority of apprentices were not receiving the minimum required level of training, and as noted in Chapter 2, nearly one in five apprentices was paid less than the minimum required wage. The largest private provider of apprentice programmes in England received an 'inadequate' rating in an Ofsted report, and will lose government funding as a result (FE Week, 2017). Poor quality, in one form or another, is one of the major challenges facing English apprenticeships.

The key new quality institution is the Institute for Apprenticeships (IfA)

The IfA formally came into existence in April 2017, simultaneously with the introduction of the apprentice levy. It is envisaged as an employer-led body, with some independence from government, and will have as a very central part of its mission the quality of apprenticeships. Most directly, the IfA will develop quality criteria, and use them to approve apprenticeship standards and assessment plans, and ensure the quality assurance of end-point assessments (IfA, 2017).

Developing quality assurance in the context of rapid change

Wholesale reform in the apprenticeship system implies new requirements for quality assurance

The shift from apprenticeship frameworks to standards, to be achieved by 2020, alongside the introduction of the apprenticeship levy and associated funding mechanisms, mean that quality assurance will face new requirements. Under the old apprenticeship framework system, apprenticeship was and is quality assured by the DfE in setting policy, Ofqual in agreeing to the qualification and an associated assessment developed by the awarding body; the Skills Funding Agency in 'accrediting' the training provider by placing it in a register of approved providers; and Ofsted in examining individual training providers and employers other than employer-providers (if only on a sample basis). Under the new standards, while there is some continuity in the role of the Department and Ofsted, key new issues are that:

- The IfA will regulate the quality of apprenticeship standards and assessments, advise government on the funding of training and assessment against apprenticeship standards, and from 2018 will have wider responsibilities to include the technical education qualifications (see IfA, 2017).
- The Education and Skills Funding Agency ESFA (successor to the SFA and EFA) will be responsible for registers of apprenticeship training providers and assessment organisations, as well as running the National Apprenticeship Service (NAS).

Quality assurance will be challenging given change and growth

Inevitably, the new standards will have teething problems – so that some features of standards that looked sensible initially will turn out to have problems. Similarly, in implementing the standards in training, some providers will pursue teaching approaches which turn out not to work well. Quality assurance capacity in the IfA and in Ofsted will need to be developed over time, gradually learning about the potential pitfalls of standards and their implementation, and how they might be overcome in practice. Stakeholders presenting evidence to the parliamentary committee enquiry made this very clear (House of Commons, 2017). Few countries have attempted apprenticeship reforms of the scale and speed of England. This is because slow evolution is a common characteristic of apprenticeship systems, often reflecting the need to obtain consensus between government, employers and often trade unions on the shape and direction of change. Quality assurance systems have, for the same reasons, also developed slowly, allowing time for the necessary expertise to be developed, issues to be identified and problems ironed out.

But the quality of apprenticeship must be assured

One of the greatest challenges in apprenticeship policy will therefore be to ensure high quality at a time of rapid change and reform. As argued in Chapter 1, careful prioritisation will be necessary to ensure that key challenges are addressed, while other longer-term requirements are addressed more gradually. But as Chapter 1 also argues, regardless of the pressures, some quality issues cannot be postponed. The whole rationale for the range of current reforms is to replace weak training options with good quality apprenticeships. If quality in the new apprenticeship system cannot be effectively ensured, that rationale collapses. The policy issues addressed below fall into the category of those which cannot be postponed.

One very important dimension of quality is equity

In England, a successful high-quality system will necessarily be inclusive, and offer routes to good jobs for vulnerable and disadvantaged groups. For example, the European EQAVET indicators of quality in vocational education and training rightly include equity measures, including completion rates and the inclusion of disadvantaged groups (European Commission, 2014). These challenges are addressed in Chapter 6.

Policy issue 5.1: Delivering a coherent apprenticeship qualifications system

Challenge: Managing the changing landscape of apprentice qualifications

Reform is changing both apprenticeship and other vocational qualifications

One key element of quality is not simply the content of individual apprentice qualifications, but also their ability to play a sensible role within a wider education and training system, complementing other qualifications, and helping to provide a coherent offer to potential students. The introduction of apprentice standards, alongside a wider qualification reform following the Sainsbury review, imply a reorganisation of the apprentice qualifications system, and their relationship to other qualifications.

Reform offers a promising opportunity to clarify the offer

By common consent England has suffered a difficult history of proliferating, overlapping and over-numerous vocational qualifications, with the then Skills Minister, Robert Halfon, reporting to parliament that current reforms seek to simplify a "spaghetti junction of qualifications" (Hansard, 2017). Following the Sainsbury and Richard reviews, the government is implementing, both for school-based and apprentice qualifications in the form of standards, the welcome principle that there should be just one qualification for each target occupation, rather than competing qualifications offered by different awarding bodies. This reflects the recommendation of a previous OECD review (Musset and Field, 2013).

But challenges are emerging in implementation

While the overarching logic of reform is clear, challenges are emerging in implementation. These challenges relate both to the number of apprentice qualifications and their relationship to wider qualifications.

Policy pointer 5.1: Delivering a coherent apprenticeship qualifications system

A credible and robust system of apprentice qualifications needs to be coherent with the wider system of vocational qualifications and manageable in number. International experience offers some guidance:

- Apprentice standards represent the requirements for the target occupation, and should therefore be closely articulated with any related technical qualification. One option would be to require all graduates of associated technical qualifications to take the apprenticeship exam to certify their occupational competence. A second option would be to establish a technical qualification as a preparatory programme for a linked apprenticeship.

- To ensure the transferability of skills, the IfA needs to ensure that each proposed standard represents a wide occupational field and therefore reject proposals that do not do so, aiming to keep the eventual total number of standards well under one thousand.
- In the context of upskilling adult learners, a more effective framework for recognising prior learning needs to be developed within the frame of apprenticeship standards and levy funding. This will need to support the top-up training and assessments for those who are able to pass the end-point assessment, but have not pursued regular apprenticeships.

Analysis: Alignment between apprenticeship and other vocational qualifications

There are three ways in which apprentice qualifications may relate to other vocational qualifications

Apprenticeship qualifications are normally linked to wider education and training qualifications. This allows both students and employers to see where apprenticeship fits within an educational progression, and what jobs and careers might result from a given apprenticeship. For any given target occupation, there are three possible ways of articulating apprentice qualifications with other vocational and educational qualifications.

- First, the target occupation, and the competences it requires, may determine whether these competences should be acquired through an apprenticeship or through some other more appropriate form of training, recognising a **division of labour** between apprenticeship and other forms of training.
- Second, there may be **alternative routes** to the same target occupation, allowing apprenticeship to offer one way of acquiring the competences, while other routes are also possible, including school or college-based training. This model is often associated with a competence-based final assessment, permitting different means of preparing for that assessment. For example, in the Netherlands there is both a school-based and an apprenticeship route to every upper secondary vocational qualification.
- Third, there may be **sequential programmes.** For example, in Norway apprentices spend the first two years of their programme in school-based upper secondary education with a relatively broad curriculum, followed normally by two years with an employer, gaining the work-based experience that will allow them to qualify as an apprentice. (Some students also continue in a school-based path after their first two years and graduate in that way).

The logic of current reforms in England implies the 'alternative routes' model, but uncertainty remains

The Sainsbury review refers to two alternative modes of vocational study at the same level, alongside a new emphasis on having only one qualification for each occupation. This seems to imply an adherence to the alternative routes approach (Independent Panel on Technical Education, 2016). The government's post-16 skills plan states there will be "only one approved tech level qualification for each occupation or cluster of occupations within a route. These tech levels could play a role within the relevant apprenticeships, but only if employers decide that should be the case, and the Institute will need to consider the implications of this single tech level approach." (BIS, 2016). This wording leaves some uncertainty. At the level of degree apprenticeships, there would, of course, still be two routes to the degree – a traditional university degree programme, and a degree apprenticeship.

Apprenticeships need to be very closely aligned with related vocational qualifications

A close alignment between apprenticeship standards and any associated technical qualifications reflects the logic and the spirit of the Sainsbury review, and best international practice. The responsibility of the Institute for Apprenticeships in ensuring that close alignment is therefore very much to be welcomed. Once an industry sector has defined the required competences for an occupation in the form of an apprenticeship standard, it would make no sense to reinvent that standard in different *occupational* requirements for a T-level qualification, (although such a qualification could reasonably include some additional cross-curricular competences). There are real risks of fragmentation, for example if there emerge slightly different qualifications, alongside apprenticeship, offering a confusing landscape of competing possibilities for the student, and indeed the employer. It is precisely this landscape of confusion, which, by common consent has been one of the weakest points in the English vocational training system, which current reforms are designed to tackle. The models for alignment in the Netherlands and Estonia offer possible models.

The Estonian system offers one option which could be applied in England

Pursuing the Estonian model, for each occupation there would be an examination – in effect the end-point assessment linked to the apprenticeship standard. Passing this examination might then offer the industry-recognised credential for the occupation, since it corresponds to a standard developed by employers in the sector. This same examination might then be pursued not only by apprentices, but also those that have been prepared for the examination – by taking a related T-level, and perhaps in other ways. Those completing T-level qualifications might be encouraged or indeed (as in Estonia) required to take the assessment examination. The principle would be that there is a single standard, defined in the apprenticeship standard and associated assessment plan by employers in the sector, and this should underpin the content of both apprenticeship and technical school-based programmes in the relevant field.

Alternatively, there could be a sequential approach

Chapter 2 showed that there is very limited general education, including basic skills, in English youth apprenticeships relative to many other countries. As suggested in that Chapter, one potential way of addressing that challenge, as well as articulating apprenticeship relative to T-levels, would be to define relevant T-levels as programmes to be pursued prior to entering apprenticeship, allowing general education to be pursued in the T-level followed by a narrower approach on occupational skills during the apprenticeship. This approach also has several attractions.

A clearer place for recognition of prior learning needs to be found

It has been widely recognised, in the Richard review and many other contexts, that in the past some so-called apprenticeships had degenerated into a simple exercise in recognition of existing skills, and current arrangements are designed to preclude that possibility. But the Richard review also argued that for those who already have the required skills, it should be possible to pursue the end-point assessment without having to go through an unnecessary apprenticeship programme (Richard, 2012). The OECD endorses that view, as this possibility of direct access to the end-point assessment, and the associated qualification, potentially represents an important route for certifying and making transparent those skills which have been acquired informally, recognising that in England most apprentices have work experience, and many will therefore already have some or even all of the competences necessary for the end-point assessment. Box 5.2 sets out how, in Australia and Denmark among many countries, apprenticeships may be completed on accelerated timetables, and how in Germany, an apprentice qualification can be acquired without pursuing an actual apprenticeship. These are two distinct options, depending on whether they do or do not involve an apprenticeship programme.

Box 5.1. Apprenticeship and school-based routes to the same qualification in the Netherlands and Estonia

In the Netherlands, the upper secondary vocational system (MBO) includes two parallel structures: an apprenticeship track (Beroepsbegeleidende Leerweg or BBL) and a school-based track (Beroepsopleidende Leerweg or BOL). Both tracks combine learning and working. In the apprenticeship track, at least 60% of the learning takes place in the workplace, often in the form of around one day of formal schooling and four days in the workplace. The school-based track includes at least 20% of workplace training and typically around 30%. Both tracks lead to the same qualifications. Participants in the school-based pathway are mainly youngsters, while almost 50% of those following a dual pathway are 24 or over. A contract (an employment contract in most cases) with a firm is mandatory to enrol in the dual/apprenticeship track. There is no such obligation for the school-based track.

In Estonia, just over 500 occupational standards, setting out the competences required for each occupation and developed by industry sectors, lightly regulated but with the co-operation of government, provide the foundation of the vocational system. Each standard is reviewed and updated every five years, and more often when necessary. Examinations to test realisation of the standard are developed and administered by 100 ‘awarding bodies’ (typically industry professional groups), granted the authority to run the examinations for a five-year period by government in consultation with the relevant industry sector and with government. Fees are regulated. These examinations form a required end- point assessment for all vocational programmes, (except those where there is no relevant examination). In upper secondary vocational programmes for example, there is a school-based test leading to the award of an upper secondary diploma, but all students are also required to take the occupational examination, and only two-thirds of them pass this typically more demanding test. These occupational examinations can be the end-point of quite different types of programme - an apprenticeship, or a school-based full-time programme for a young person, or a part-time programme for an adult – or the examination may be pursued without formal preparation by someone who has acquired the relevant competences working in the occupation.

Source: Fazekas, M. and I. Litjens (2014), *A Skills beyond School Review of the Netherlands*, OECD Reviews of Vocational Education and Training, OECD Publishing. http://dx.doi.org/10.1787/9789264221840-en.

Box 5.2. Recognition of prior learning in apprenticeships: Accelerated completion and qualification without taking the apprenticeship programme

In Australia, apprentices may receive course credits for skills they already have and their prior work experience, reducing training duration. The apprenticeship contract defines a nominal term, which can be reduced (or extended), as all apprenticeships are "competency based". If an apprentice can demonstrate that they have acquired the required skill level, they may progress to the next stage of their training or complete the apprenticeship. Competency is assessed first by the "registered training organisation" (training provider). Then employers need to confirm that the apprentice is able to apply the same skills in the workplace.

Source: Australian Apprenticeships (2017), "For employers", www.australianapprenticeships.gov.au/employers (accessed 30 August 2017); State Government of Victoria, Australia (2017), "TAFE and training", www.education.vic.gov.au/training/Pages/default.aspx (accessed 30 August 2017).

In Denmark, Adults aged 25 and above may complete an apprenticeship through two alternative pathways, in addition to the regular apprenticeship programme. They first undergo individual competence assessment (which lasts between half a day and ten days), which determines which pathway they may follow. Those with at least two years of relevant experience are exempted from the basic course (which includes school-based vocational training), and follow a shortened main course (which normally combines school-based and company-based training) and do not need on-the-job training. Those with some relevant work experience or prior education and training may follow a shortened basic course (up to 20 weeks), a shortened main course and up to two years of on-the-job training.

Source: Danish Ministry of Higher Education and Science (2017), "Admission to vocational education and training (VET)", https://ufm.dk/en/education-and-institutions/recognition-and-transparency/recognition-guide/admission-vet (accessed 30 August 2017).

In Germany, individuals may take an "external examination" (Externenprüfung), involving the final assessment of regular apprenticeship programmes without completing the programme itself. Access to this exam is limited to those who have worked in the target occupation at least for one and a half times as long as the duration of the apprenticeship, and they have been performing skilled tasks in their job. Relevant school qualifications may reduce or replace the required minimum work experience. Candidates may prepare for the assessment by themselves (e.g. taking tests from past years, reading the technical literature as proposed by websites that advise potential candidates) or following preparatory courses. In 2009 candidates who took the external examination accounted for 6.4% of successful apprenticeship final assessment candidates.

Source: BIBB (2017), "Externenprüfung: Voraussetzungen, Beratung und Vorbereitung" www.perspektive-berufsabschluss.de/de/501.php (accessed 30 August 2017).

While SFA funding rules allow for recognition of prior learning, their practical application will be challenging

SFA funding rules require the cost, content and duration of an individual apprenticeship to take full account of prior learning, so that it should not be possible to offer funding to learn skills which the apprentices already have (SFA, 2017). For example, the apprenticeship standard for equine groom includes many competences which someone familiar with horses may be expected to have already, but as a Level 2 apprenticeship occupying 12-18 months, with a minimum apprenticeship length of 12 months, it will be very difficult to address the needs of an experienced person, who needs no more than a top-up of skills and knowledge to realise the standard, or indeed those capable of succeeding immediately in an end-point assessment (see GOV.UK, 2017). If such individuals are shoehorned into full 12 month minimum apprenticeships, this will be wasteful. Equally, employers may not wish to offer apprenticeships, with 20% off-the-job training, to their employees if those employees are already close to fully skilled. The needs of individuals in these circumstances need to be addressed in some other way, leading to an end-point assessment similar to that offered in Germany. At present in England, there is no framework for supporting top-up training, or for the assessments, for those in this position. Nor is there the nomenclature in place to describe the qualification that would be obtained by such a person – although this could easily be rectified, for example by granting all those who successfully pass the end-point assessment a 'diploma' in that occupation, that might not always arise from an apprenticeship. Such a framework, allowing apprenticeship qualifications to be used to recognise prior learning, needs to be developed, recognising that those concerned will not be apprentices, and could not therefore be funded under the standard rules for apprentices.

Analysis: Defining the number of apprenticeship standards

Other countries have limited number of apprenticeship standards

Other countries with strong apprenticeship systems typically manage with a relatively limited number of apprentice training occupations. In Austria, Switzerland and Germany, although half or more of the youth cohort enter apprenticeship, the number of apprentice standards is between two and three hundred in each country (Bliem et al., 2016). In Ontario in Canada, apprenticeships are available in 150 skilled trades (Government of Ontario, n.d.). In Estonia, there are just over 500 occupational standards, and all apprenticeships need to be directed at one or other of these standards. In Denmark apprenticeship may be pursued in 111 different fields, at various levels in each field (European Commission, n.d.). Sometimes a specialisation may be permitted within an apprenticeship, without removing the main title of the qualification.

Pressures from employers to create overly narrow apprentice standards are to be expected

As set out in OECD (2010), employers in a specific occupational and industrial niche sector naturally want to develop the skills of those working in the sector, but do not want to lose those skills through mobility to other sectors, even in related sectors where skills requirements are similar. Apprentice qualifications, drawn narrowly to fit the niche sector alone, serve to protect the interests of employers in the niche sector, but by the same token can be an artificial barrier to labour market mobility, because they disguise the extent to which the skillset is transferable to other similar occupations. In the interests of apprentices, and the labour market as a whole, the IfA therefore needs to insist on broad apprentice standards, even if this slows down the replacement of frameworks by standards. In some countries – for example Austria - the involvement of trade unions in agreeing new training occupations balances employer interests, since trade unions, with an eye on the careers of their members, are typically interested in ensuring that apprentice graduates can work in a broad industrial sector. In Austria, the outcome of social partnership negotiation of individual apprenticeship profiles results in a fruitful compromise between meeting very specific employer needs and the longer-term career interests of the graduate apprentices (see Hoeckel, 2010).

Narrow apprentice standards will multiply the burdens on the IfA and employers

Every apprentice standard needs to be updated periodically in consultation with employers. Engaging employers in this task may be much harder than creating a standard, particularly in cases where employer consultation is necessary to pursue the unexciting but essential work of winding up redundant standards, or merging them into other standards. Each standard also requires bodies not only to provide training, but also to provide assessments – and this latter task is already a challenge. This needs to be pursued carefully and with adequate resources, both in the IfA, and on the employer side, to maintain quality in the apprenticeship system. The greater the number of standards the harder this task will be.

It is worrying that 500 apprentice standards are already under development

The IfA is already reporting concerns that some standards may be overlapping or amount to micro-qualifications (IfA, 2017). Some of those giving evidence to the House of Commons select committee suggested that as many as 1 500 apprenticeship standards may emerge, many times more than in comparable countries (as indicated above), and increasing the confusion for employers and learners (House of Commons, 2017). The narrowness of standards suggested by these numbers implies difficulty for the graduate apprentice in career development, challenges because of the burden of updating such a large number of standards, and greater difficulty in recruiting appropriate assessment bodies. It will also make apprenticeships less attractive by narrowing career opportunities for apprentice graduates. Taken together, these problems could seriously damage the apprenticeship system in England.

Policy issue 5.2: Ensuring reliable end-point assessments

Challenge: Thinking through the effects of markets in the provision of assessment

End-point assessments represent one of the key elements of quality assurance

In England, the new apprenticeship standards are attached to an assessment plan setting out the elements of the final assessment – paper and pencil examinations, interviews and practical tests. End-point assessments take place once the individual employer of the apprentices is satisfied that the apprentice has acquired all the relevant competences. The function of the end-point assessment is therefore to ensure that the confidence of the individual employer in the skills of the apprentice can be backed by an external and objective quality check. Such a check is in effect quality assurance, on behalf of employers and apprentice graduates more generally, that the skills of this individual apprentice graduate are up to the standard expected in the industry. It is envisaged that there will be a market in how assessments are conducted. So, while the post-Sainsbury reforms have eliminated competition in the market offering qualifications in favour of regulated monopolies subject to a franchise competition, an open market in the delivery of assessments will remain.

Policy pointer 5.2: Ensuring reliable end-point assessments

Few, if any, other countries seek to achieve consistency in assessment standards through multiple bodies conducting the assessment and consistency in standards will be impossible to achieve with current plans for multiple assessment bodies for individual standards. Given the key role of consistent assessment standards in the credibility and reputation of apprentice qualifications these plans should be reviewed.

Analysis: The impact of competition

Most other countries maintain one assessment body per assessment

Looked at across countries, there are few or no directly comparable systems, in which there is the possibility of choosing between competing assessment bodies to deliver the same final assessment. In the English context, it may not seem unusual to have such competition, given the history of regulated but quite open markets in the development of qualifications and associated assessments by awarding bodies. But one of the effects of the Sainsbury review is to move away from this model, at least in respect of qualifications, given a history of qualification proliferation, quality problems and potentially a race to the bottom in standards.

Several countries balance flexibility in how skills are acquired with single final assessments

The well-regarded Swiss post-secondary vocational education and training (VET) system allows a very open and competitive market in training providers, preparing students for the professional examinations, but there is a single examination, organised nationally under the aegis of employers, but subject to light touch federal regulation (see Fazekas and Field, 2013). A different example lies in the Dutch school system, which, by PISA standards at least achieves outstanding results with no national curriculum, and with schools that have extensive autonomy over how they teach, but subject to single national examinations. The principle in all these cases is that the single end-point assessment, administered by a single body, provides a counterbalancing form of quality assurance and accountability to an open market and choice in the forms of learning that lead to that end-point assessment (OECD, 2016).

Sometimes there will be little competition in the provision of assessments

For some, possibly many apprenticeship standards, it is already clear that there may be few bodies willing to offer assessments (see House of Commons, 2017). In these cases, the task of quality assurance will become that of ensuring that there is at least one provider of assessments, and regulating that provider. This task would be easier if single provision were built into the design of the system.

More common apprenticeships will involve competition between assessment providers

There will be little price competition in the market for assessment providers, given that employers that have not exhausted their levy pots will be relatively indifferent to price, while those that cannot draw on a levy pot will only have to pay 10% of the cost. Assessment providers will instead compete very narrowly on different approaches to exam questions and the training of assessors. At the same time, assessment bodies and the way in which they go about their work will inevitably have some influence on the pass threshold. This is worrying on two grounds. First, the incentives falling on an employer in choosing an assessment body will be to choose a body which is unlikely to challenge the judgement of that employer that an apprentice is ready to graduate. Providers, who may advise on the choice of assessor, will also not wish to see an apprentice that they have trained fail the assessment, not least as providers are judged on successful completions. Second, while there is no single objectively 'right' pass threshold, it is undesirable for such thresholds to vary between different assessment bodies, and such variability is inevitable given multiple assessment bodies.

Multiple assessment providers will lead to inconsistent assessment standards

A practical example highlights the problem. The assessment plan for the adult care worker apprenticeship standard includes a 'judgement test' and a 'professional discussion'. The judgement test poses 60 multiple choice questions on real life scenarios. Achieving the 40 correct answers required for a pass clearly depends on the choice of questions and scenarios. Equally, the standardised interview template for the more open-ended professional discussion cannot avoid an element of subjective judgement on the part of the assessor. This is no criticism of the assessment plan, but it underlines the fact that consistent application of a pass standard is demanding, and even if just one assessment body is responsible, consistency between different tests at different points in time and different assessors presents many challenges – a challenge discussed in the context of educational testing in terms of test 'reliability' (Wells and Wollack, 2003). But a single assessment body could take clear responsibility for consistency/reliability, and address it by using common question banks and sets of scenarios for multiple choice questions, and by ensuring that assessors are similarly trained, and meet regularly to discuss the formal and informal criteria applied in the professional discussion, and converge their approaches. Multiple competing assessment bodies will make such convergence impossible. Any supposed overarching quality assurance will remain beside the point in the absence of a credible methodology for delivering consistency/reliability. In fact the terminology of 'quality assurance' misses the target: two good quality assessments can have inconsistent pass thresholds.

Many informed stakeholders are concerned about consistency in end-point assessments

The recent report by the parliamentary select committee, and evidence given to that committee by a wide variety of well-informed stakeholders including Ofsted, the Association of Colleges, and the organisations of awarding bodies, has underlined the serious challenges of ensuring consistency/validity in assessment standards, challenges which in the view of the select committee could not be adequately addressed by the proposed quality assurance arrangements (House of Commons, 2017). The OECD shares that view. The logical conclusion is that the challenge of consistency would be much easier to handle if England followed the well-established model of other countries, and franchised a single assessment body for each apprenticeship standard, or group of standards. As with vocational qualifications, some contestability should be preserved by franchising the body responsible for assessment in relation to a particular occupational standard for a limited period – say five years.

References

BIS (Department of Business, Innovation and Skills) (2016), *Post-16 Skills Plan*, BIS, www.gov.uk/government/uploads/system/uploads/attachment_data/file/536068/56259_Cm_9280_print.pdf.

BIS (2014), "Apprenticeships evaluation: Learner survey", *BIS Research Paper*, No. 205, www.gov.uk/government/publications/apprenticeships-evaluation-learner-survey-2014.

Bliem, W., A. Petanovitsch and K. Schmid (2016), *Dual Vocational Education and Training in Austria, Germany, Liechtenstein and Switzerland,* Institut für Bildungsforschung der Wirtschaft, www.dcdualvet.org/wp-content/uploads/Dual-VET-Comparative-Study_Full-Study.pdf.

Broek, S. and B.-J. Buiskool (2013), *Developing the Adult Learning Sector: Quality in the Adult Learning Sector (Lot 1),* Final Report (Open Call for tender EAC/26/2011), Panteia, Zoetermeer, http://arhiv.acs.si/porocila/Quality_in_the_Adult_Learning_Sector-final_report.pdf.

DfE (Department for Education) (2017), "Register of apprenticeship training providers", www.gov.uk/government/uploads/system/uploads/attachment_data/file/562465/Provider_register_policy_doc.pdf.

European Commission (2014), *Report from The Commission To The European Parliament And The Council,* European Commission, Brussels, http://ec.europa.eu/dgs/education_culture/repository/education/policy/vocational-policy/doc/eqavet_en.pdf.

European Commission (2009), *Recommendation of the European Parliament and of the Council of 18 June 2009 on the establishment of a European Quality Assurance Reference Framework for Vocational Education and Training.*

European Commission (n.d.) , *Apprenticeship Toolbox*, www.apprenticeship-toolbox.eu/.

European Training Foundation (2014), *Quality Assurance in Vocational Education and Training a Collection of Articles,* European Training Foundation, www.etf.europa.eu/webatt.nsf/0/270970490A6E9327C1257CA800407038/$file/Quality%20assurance%20in%20VET.pdf.

Fazekas, M. and S. Field (2013), A *Skills beyond School Review of Switzerland*, OECD Reviews of Vocational Education and Training, OECD Publishing, Paris, http://dx.doi.org/10.1787/9789264062665-en.

GOV.UK (2017), "Guidance. Search for apprenticeship standards. New apprenticeship standards are developed by employer groups known as 'trailblazers', published 3 November 2017, www.gov.uk/guidancesearch-for-apprenticeship-standards.

Government of Ontario (n.d.), "Start and apprenticeship", www.ontario.ca/page/start-apprenticeship#section-3.

Hansard, House of Commons (2017), 27 March 2017. Evidence given by Robert Halfon Minister for Apprenticeships and Skills, https://hansard.parliament.uk/commons/2017-03-27/debates/8baab83a-aa21-4419-9313-efe97dcbb520/DraftPublicSectorApprenticeshipTargetsRegulations2017.

Hoeckel, K. (2010), *OECD Reviews of Vocational Education and Training: A Learning for Jobs Review of Austria 2010*, OECD Publishing, Paris, http://dx.doi.org/10.1787/9789264113695-en.

House of Commons (2017), *Apprenticeships,* Business, Energy and Industrial Strategy and Education Committees Sub Committee on Education, Skills and the Economy, www.publications.parliament.uk/pa/cm201617/cmselect/cmese/206/206.pdf.

Independent Panel on Technical Education (2016), *Report of the Independent Panel on Technical Education,* www.gatsby.org.uk/uploads/education/reports/pdf/report-of-the-independent-panel-on-technical-education1.pdf.

Institute for Apprenticeships (2017a), *Driving the Quality of Apprenticeships in England,* https://media.wix.com/ugd/4971f0_66f9a66ab82f456b97ce5fc656b923d1.pdf.

Institute for Apprenticeships (2017b), *Driving the Quality of Apprenticeships in England (Institute for Apprenticeships operational plan),* www.gov.uk/government/uploads/system/uploads/attachment_data/file/609008/IfA_Driving_Quality_.pdf.

Institute for Apprenticeships (2016), *Adult Care Worker Assessment Strategy*, www.gov.uk/government/uploads/system/uploads/attachment_data/file/539997/ACW_Assessment_plan.pdf.

Kis V. (forthcoming), "Making skills transparent: Recognising vocational skills acquired through work-based learning", *OECD Education Working Papers*, OECD Publishing, Paris.

Kis, V. (2010), *OECD Reviews of Vocational Education and Training: A Learning for Jobs Review of Ireland 2010*, OECD Publishing, Paris, http://dx.doi.org/10.1787/9789264113848-en.

Musset, P. and S. Field (2013), *A Skills beyond School Review of England*, OECD Reviews of Vocational Education and Training, OECD Publishing, Paris, http://dx.doi.org/10.1787/9789264203594-en.

OECD (2016), *Netherlands 2016: Foundations for the Future*, OECD Publishing, Paris, http://dx.doi.org/10.1787/9789264257658-en.

OECD (2010), *Learning for Jobs*, OECD Publishing, Paris, http://dx.doi.org/10.1787/9789264087460-en.

Ofsted (2017), *Further Education and Skills Inspection Handbook*, www.gov.uk/government/uploads/system/uploads/attachment_data/file/608481/Further_education_and_skills_inspection_handbook_for_use_from_April_2017.pdf.

Ofsted (2015), *Apprenticeships: Developing Skills for Future Prosperity: How Well Do Apprenticeships Meet The Needs of Young People, Their Employers And The Economy*?

Pilz, M. (2012), "Modularisation of vocational training in Germany, Austria and Switzerland: Parallels and disparities in a modernisation process", *Journal of Vocational Education & Training*, Vol. 64/2, pp.69-183, http://dx.doi.org/10.1080/13636820.2011.628757.

Richard, D. (2012), *The Richard Review of Apprenticeships,* School for Startups, London, United Kingdom, www.gov.uk/government/uploads/system/uploads/attachment_data/file/34708/richard-review-full.pdf.

Sweet, R. (2014), *Work-based Learning: A Handbook for Policy Makers and Social Partners in ETF Partner Countries*, http://ec.europa.eu/education/library/publications/etf-wbl-handbook_en.pdf.

U.S. Congress, Office of Technology Assessment (1994), *Testing and Assessment in Vocational Education, OTA-BP-SET-123*, Government Printing Office, Washington, DC, United States, http://ota.fas.org/reports/9437.pdf.

Ulicna, D. and A. Curth (2013), *Study on Quality Assurance in Continuous VET and on Future Development of EQAVET*, Final Report, ICF GHK, Brussels, www.eqavet.eu/Libraries/2014_Publications/Study_on_QA_in_CVET.sflb.ashx.

Wells, C. and J. Wollack (2003), *An Instructor's Guide to Understanding Test Reliability,* Testing & Evaluation Services, University of Wisconsin, https://testing.wisc.edu/Reliability.pdf.

Chapter 6. Equity and inclusion in apprenticeship in England

Recent reforms of apprenticeship in England have not usually taken equity as an explicit objective, apart from some special measures and targets such as for minority group participation. Instead, the emphasis has been on establishing a high-quality, high status apprenticeship brand, with higher-level apprenticeships. While the objective of these reforms is commendable, they could risk leaving behind some weaker performers who will find it harder to obtain and complete more demanding apprenticeships. This chapter argues that building on the experience of traineeships, England should further explore, in the light of evidence and experience, pre-apprenticeship and alternative apprenticeship programmes that effectively prepare young people to undertake a full apprenticeship, equip them with basic and employability skills, and grant them workplace experience and career advice.

Introduction: Equity and apprenticeship policy

How apprenticeship reform in England bears on social mobility

In principle apprenticeships should be a vehicle for social mobility

In England, one effect of the wide-ranging apprenticeship reforms is to identify apprenticeship as one of the main potential routes by which young people may gain access to good jobs and careers. Given this expanded role, it may be expected that apprenticeship should contribute to social mobility, by facilitating the advance of young people from disadvantaged backgrounds into rewarding careers. This aspiration is supported by international experience, which shows, for example, that countries with strong dual system apprenticeship systems have lower rates of NEET among young people (Quintini and Martin, 2006).

But realising this aspiration involves significant challenges

Apprenticeships have often, at least up to now, involved relatively low-level qualifications, and often in fields of study characterised by low pay. The most desirable, higher-level apprenticeships (Level 4 and 5) leading to well paid jobs have mostly been filled by older apprentices aged 25 and above (DfE, 2016). The majority of these higher-level apprentices were white, similarly to Level 2 and 3 apprentices (DfE, 2016). Alongside the more general equity challenges, some groups, including minorities, may therefore face particular obstacles in apprenticeship (see for example Beck at al., 2006a; Beck at al., 2006b; Fuller and Unwin, 2014).

Moving apprenticeship upmarket may advance the labour market prospects of some

Apart from some special measures and targets such as for minority group participation, recent reforms to apprenticeship have not usually taken equity as an explicit objective. Instead, the emphasis has been on establishing a high-quality, high status apprenticeship brand, with higher-level apprenticeships. While the objective of these reforms is commendable, they could risk leaving behind some weaker performers who will find it harder to obtain and complete more demanding apprenticeships.

England has more young people with weak basic skills than other countries

In England in 2012 approaching one-third (29%) of 16-24 year-olds had weak basic skills in the sense of numeracy and/or literacy below Level 2 in the PIAAC survey, one of the highest levels among OECD countries in the survey, and three times the level of a strong performer like the Netherlands (9%) and substantially more than – say – Germany (19%). While those from less advantaged family backgrounds are everywhere more likely to suffer from weak basic skills, this factor of inheritance is stronger in England than in most other countries (see Kuczera, Field and Windisch, 2016). School reforms are addressing weakness in initial basic skills acquisition, but any improvements will take some time. In the short run, it would be very unfortunate if this group of poorly skilled school leavers was left behind by a move 'upmarket' of apprenticeship and other vocational qualifications. To meet this challenge, England needs measures to engage these young people through apprenticeships as well as in other ways. This means finding effective ways of preparing young people at risk so that they have the skills to gain an apprenticeship place, supporting them through to successful completion, and ensuring that the apprenticeship can lead to higher levels of qualification and a rewarding career.

Profound challenges lie on the demand side

As well as creating demanding, high status apprentice qualifications, employers will need to offer apprenticeships to young people with weak basic skills who may not present themselves as the most attractive candidates. Chapter 2, in the context of youth apprenticeship, describes a range of changes in the labour market faced by young people, which mean that low-skilled young people entering the labour market are very often under-employed, or in insecure or temporary work, and therefore without a career ladder. Collectively these changes are placing an increasing segment of the labour force, particularly young people, outside the longer-term relationship between employer and employee that might favour an employer's commitment to training. Many studies (e.g. Keep and James, 2011) argue that major challenges in England lie on the demand side, with many employers having an entrenched reliance on substantial numbers of low-skilled workers and few incentives to promote their upskilling. These labour market factors, unless they are separately addressed, may put a substantial brake on the capacity of the education and training system, including apprenticeship, to deliver career advance to young people.

How other countries address equity through apprenticeship

Countries address the challenge both before and during apprenticeships

Other countries have sought to build inclusive apprenticeship systems, mainly through additional preparation for disadvantaged young people to enable them to enter apprenticeships, and targeted support during apprenticeships to help them through to successful completion. This chapter looks at these issues, and draws extensively on a recent OECD survey of work-based learning as a means of supporting school to work transition (Kis, 2016). Countries have approached equity in apprenticeship systems using several policy tools as set out below. The first three bullet points will be considered in more depth in the policy discussion which follows. The fourth bullet point, on financial incentives, is looked at briefly here.

- Pre-apprenticeship schemes designed to prepare young people for good quality apprenticeships leading to rewarding careers. Such pre-apprenticeship schemes are not necessarily always designed for those at risk – sometimes they may also meet the needs of those who, for one reason or another, need preparation before entering apprenticeship. In some contexts, pre-apprenticeship may be a near-universal stage that young people pass through before entering full apprenticeships.
- Special forms of apprenticeship are sometimes used to include young people at risk. Often, they may be designed so as to encourage participants to transition into regular apprenticeship, and in this sense they are also a form of pre-apprenticeship. But usually they also allow for graduation within the special apprenticeship scheme, offering a qualification with labour market value.
- Programmes of support during apprenticeships to assist apprentices to cope with and succeed in demanding training programmes.
- Direct financial incentives to providers and/or employers to take apprentices from disadvantaged backgrounds.

Some countries offer financial incentives

Incentives may be offered to employers to take on apprentices from certain designated equity groups (see Box 6.1). In England, providers currently receive an additional GBP 600 for training on a framework an apprentice who lives in the top 10% of deprived areas (as per the Index of Multiple Deprivation), GBP 300 for any apprentice who lives in the next

10% of deprived areas (the 10-20% range), and GBP 200 for those in the next 7% (the 20-27% range).

But there is a risk of subsidising training that would have been offered anyway

While targeted financial assistance seems appealing, it is hard to get right. For example, in Germany a training bonus scheme targeted youth who had unsuccessfully applied for an apprenticeship, had lower secondary schooling or less, or had learning difficulties or a disability (Bonin et al., 2013). Employers received between EUR 4 000 and 6 000 per additional apprentice, half of which was paid after a four-month probationary period and half when the apprentice took their final exam. The bonus was available to employers where the number of apprenticeship positions, including disadvantaged apprentices, was higher than on average during the preceding three years. For hiring disabled apprentices, a firm could receive an additional 30%. But evaluation (Bonin et al., 2013) found that over 90% of subsidised apprentices would have been hired even without the bonus. Employers reported that better basic skills among applicants and more support for weaker apprentices during training would be more helpful than a subsidy. Müehlemann (2016) argues that the bonus for disadvantaged apprentices was too low to make a difference, and that it would be hard to define an effective level of subsidy. This reflects the problem of cost-benefit heterogeneity, discussed in Chapter 4.

Box 6.1. Incentives to employers taking disadvantaged apprentices

In Australia, employers receive AUD 1 250 when at the Certificate II level they take an apprentice who belongs to a nominated 'equity group'. Equity groups include indigenous Australians, job seekers with major barriers to employment, school-based apprentices, apprentices working in a rural or regional area, and apprentices with disabilities.

In Austria, for apprentices with learning difficulties, financial support is available to cover the costs of additionally required courses (e.g. literacy support), covering costs up to EUR 3 000 per apprentice. In addition, if the apprentice must repeat the year, employers will be compensated for the resulting extra costs (e.g. apprentice wage).

In France firms benefit from a higher tax break (EUR 2 200 instead of EUR 1 600 per apprentice) if the apprentice is disadvantaged and is in the first year of their training programme. Eligible apprentices include those who are disabled, unqualified people aged 16-25 needing support for transition into professional life, and those aged 18-22 who have signed a voluntary integration contract (*contrat de volontariat pour l'insertion*) that targets youth most disconnected from employment.

Source: Australian Government (2016), Apprenticeships website, www.australianapprenticeships.gov.au; WKO (2016), Wirtschaftskammer Österreich (Austrian Economic Chambers), "Überblick der Lehrlingsförderungen", www.wko.at; Service-Public-Pro (2016), "Crédit d'impôt apprentissage", www.service-public.fr/professionnels-entreprises.

Policy issue 6.1: Developing pre-apprenticeships and special apprenticeship schemes

Challenge: Ensuring adequate provision of pre-apprenticeships

Measures are needed to prepare young people with weak school attainment for apprenticeship

For the most desirable apprenticeships, offering good training and a rewarding career, employers will naturally seek out the most talented rather than those most in need. Often, failure to obtain a desired apprenticeship is not because of any lack of overall employer demand for apprentices, but rather because employers are reluctant to accept the candidates they are offered as they see them as lacking the basic numeracy, literacy and employability skills that will support apprenticeship learning, and translate into a valuable skilled worker in the future.

One response in many countries is preparatory programmes or 'pre-apprenticeships'

'Pre-apprenticeship' programmes, found in many countries, usually aim to develop the general, vocational and soft skills (including employability skills) that help young people to obtain and successfully complete an apprenticeship. They typically combine education in schools with elements of work-based learning. Such programmes often also offer career orientation, assisting young people understand the realities of different career options. Such orientation can help young people to refine or modify their career targets, and potential apprenticeship programme, in the light of experience. Programmes may provide credit towards a regular apprenticeship. They are called bridging programmes in Switzerland, transition programmes in Germany, and pre-apprenticeship in Australia and the United States. Table 6.1, adapted from Kis, (2016) summarises initiatives in selected OECD countries.

Such pre-apprenticeships often, but not always, are designed for young people at risk

As they are preparatory programmes, pre-apprenticeship programmes often do serve the needs of young people at risk of dropout, by re-engaging them with learning, familiarising them with working life, and preparing them for the challenges of regular apprenticeship. But they can also meet the needs of students, including able students who simply need some preparation before entering apprenticeship. Sometimes this approach is made general. For example, in Norway, the two years of school-based vocational education and training which normally precedes an apprenticeship in the form of a work placement may be conceived as a pre-apprenticeship which is pursued by all.

Special apprenticeships designed for young people at risk

Alongside programmes designed to prepare for entrance to apprenticeship, some countries offer special forms of apprenticeship designed for young people who may not be adequately prepared for regular apprenticeship or school-based options. They often (like pre-apprenticeships) channel young people into regular apprenticeships and prepare for a specific occupation by providing a lower level vocational qualification.

Traineeships in England show much promise

The Richard review argued that "a significant new offer should be introduced to support young people's transition into work, developing their employability skills, and where relevant, preparing them for a high skilled apprenticeship. The new programme – 'traineeships' perhaps - should replace existing apprenticeships where they are linked to lower skilled jobs" (Richard, 2012). In response, the traineeships now in place are designed to help young people aged 16 to 24 with the training, English, maths and work experience needed to secure an apprenticeship or employment. They typically involve 200- 400 guided learning hours of training and work experience over a period of a few months (6 months is maximum). Just under 20 000 young people started traineeships in 2014/15, growing to just over 24 000 in 2015/16, but in 2016/2017 starts decreased by 15% in comparison to the previous year (DfE, 2017). Initial process evaluation results are favourable with two-thirds of graduate trainees going on to a mix of apprenticeship (22%), employment (28%) and further learning (17%) (BIS, 2015). Of those who started or completed a traineeship in 2013/14, 59% progressed into sustained employment and 39% into sustained learning (BIS, 2015).

Such pre-apprenticeship programmes are more common and more substantial in many other countries

Given their duration and objectives, traineeships in England are classified as pre-apprenticeships, and compared with similar initiatives elsewhere. In some European countries, pre-apprenticeship is both more common than in England, and the programmes are also more substantial (with programmes usually of a *minimum* of 6 months, rather than a *maximum* of 6 months, as in English traineeships). While in England, given 24 000 trainee starts in 2015/16 there are now around 5 pre-apprentices (traineeship participants) for every 100 new apprentices, the equivalent figure for Switzerland in 2012 was 22 pre-apprentices for every 100 new apprentices, and for Germany in 2013 was 52; Landert and Eberli, 2015). For England to match this ratio with 500 000 apprentice starts per year (roughly the current figure), this would require between 100 and 250 thousand traineeships annually, between four and ten times the present figure.

Policy pointer 6.1: Developing pre-apprenticeships and special apprenticeship schemes

A key element in the success of a reformed apprenticeship system will be its capacity to include and engage those from disadvantaged backgrounds, and those who leave school with few skills. Building on the experience of traineeships, further explore, in the light of evidence and experience, pre-apprenticeship and alternative apprenticeship programmes that effectively prepare young people to undertake a full apprenticeship, equip them with basic and employability skills, and grant them workplace experience and career advice.

Analysis: International experience with pre-apprenticeships

There is a strong argument in principle for expanding and developing pre-apprenticeships

Given, as described above, a large cohort of young people in England with weak basic skills, and an expanding apprenticeship system with rising standards and demands, there is a big need to bridge the gap, with measures that transition young people into apprenticeships, including traineeships (but not necessarily limited to them). Given a limited evidence base, the precise modalities of such programmes will require development in the light of evaluation and monitoring, drawing on international experience. Since pre-apprenticeship programmes are not eligible for levy funding, effective funding arrangements will need to be in place.

Some have suggested reconfiguring some existing youth apprenticeships as pre-apprenticeship

The traineeships programme appears to be relatively successful in the light of initial evaluations, but it has not replaced lower level apprenticeships, as proposed in the Richard review. As discussed in Chapter 2 in connection with youth apprenticeships, in an IPPR study, Pullen and Dromey (2016) argue that Level 2 apprenticeships for 16-18 year-olds should be replaced by a pre-apprenticeship programme that would include more general education and a recognised qualification, and therefore be more appropriate to 16-18 year-olds.

Across countries, pre-apprenticeships, often organised locally, take diverse forms

Looked at across countries, pre-apprenticeship programmes are exceptionally diverse, partly reflecting the fact that they are often organised locally or regionally. For example, in Switzerland, some programmes are regulated at federal level and funded by unemployment insurance, while others (bridging measures) are funded by cantons and communities but supported by federal funds. Most bridging programmes are provided by public institutions, but 12% of provision is delivered by private entities (Landert and Eberli, 2015). Table 6.1 describes initiatives preparing young people for apprenticeships.

Evaluations are essential to identify what works

Hard evidence on the success or otherwise of pre-apprenticeship is patchy, and difficult to compare with alternative measures for youth at risk. Evaluations, unsurprisingly given the way in which participants are selected, suggest that pre-apprenticeship participants tend to have weaker skills and qualifications than those who choose other learning pathways, and often have higher dropout rates *(Autorengruppe Bildungsberichterstattung*, 2016; Karmel and Oliver, 2011). In Australia, pre-apprenticeship participants had higher than average completion rates of apprenticeship in construction and electro-technology, but not in engineering trades and hairdressing (Karmel and Oliver, 2011).

Table 6.1. Pre-apprenticeship programmes in selected OECD countries

Country	Programme name	Target group	Duration	Content	Regulatory framework
Australia	Pre-apprenticeship		Typically 6-12 months	General employability skills, trade skills specific to a particular apprenticeship occupation	No national definition or regulatory framework, currently no Commonwealth funding (previous funding programmes were ceased)
England (UK)	Traineeship	Youth aged 16-24 qualified below Level 3 with little work experience and not in employment (not intended for the most disengaged young people, who require intensive support)	6 weeks to 6 months	Work experience placement (100-240 hours); work preparation training (including soft skills); English and mathematics if needed	Framework for delivery defines core content and eligibility criteria. Funded by the Education Funding Agency for 16-19 year-olds and by the Adult Skills Budget for 19-24 year-olds. Exact content to be agreed between training provider and employer
Germany	Introductory training (*Einsiegsqualifizerung*), including a variant called "EQ Plus"	Youth aged 16-25. EQ Plus targets youth with learning difficulties and those socially disadvantaged	6-12 months	Work-based learning under a contract concluded with a training company. Optional school-based component. Under EQ Plus: social and educational support, additional school-based and company-based tutoring, mentoring	Regulatory framework provided by the National Training Pact. Funded by local employment agencies and job centres
	Preparatory VET year (*Berufsvorbereitungs-jahr*, BVJ)	Youth aged under 18 who completed compulsory education (including those without a lower secondary qualification)	1 year (may be extended to 18 months)	General subjects (German, mathematics, English) at vocational school (leading to a lower secondary qualification). Exploration of three occupational fields through theory and practice (including work placements)	
	Basic vocational year (*Berufsgrundbildungsjahr*, BGJ)	Youth who have obtained a lower secondary qualification	1 year	Vocational theory and practice in a particular field taught at a vocational school, with an element of work placement (either in a block or alternating two days at school and three days at work)	
Scotland (UK)	Certificate of Work Readiness	16-24 year-olds	10-12 weeks	3-4 weeks of off-the-job training (e.g. dealing with work situations, responsibilities of employment, personal development self and work and skills for customer care). 190 hours of work experience	It can be funded by the Employability Fund – Scottish Government funding administered through Skills Development Scotland

Country	Programme name	Target group	Duration	Content	Regulatory framework
Switzerland	SEMO (motivational semester)	Youth under the age of 25 who completed compulsory education	6 months (may be extended to 9.5 months)	1-2 days per week at a vocational school	Regulated by the Swiss State Secretariat for Economic Affairs, funded through unemployment insurance. Co-ordinated by cantonal labour offices. Programmes organised/delivered by sponsors (e.g. associations, foundations, labour offices etc.)
	Bridging measures	Youth who have finished lower secondary education	1 year	Language skills, mathematics, motivation and career guidance. Either school-based or combined school and work-based training. Some participants have a pre-apprenticeship contract with their training company. A special programme targets migrants	Funded by cantons and communities
United States	Pre-apprenticeship		Not specified	Literacy, mathematics, English and work-readiness skills delivered through classroom instruction and industry-based training	No mandatory framework. The Employment and Training Administration defined a pre-apprenticeship quality framework that aims to build a broader understanding of pre-apprenticeship programmes

Source: Adapted from Kis, V. (2016), "Work-based learning for youth at risk: Getting employers on board", *OECD Education Working Papers*, No. 150, http://dx.doi.org/10.1787/5e122a91-en.

Special forms of apprenticeship are targeted at youth at risk

These programmes are typically shorter than regular apprenticeships and target young people who are less academically oriented and are at risk of dropping out from the mainstream education. In Norway, shorter two-year apprenticeships (*Praksisbrev*) are provided alongside regular apprenticeships lasting four years (Norwegian Ministry of Education, n.d). Similarly, Switzerland offers two-year EBA apprenticeships (*Grundbildu ng mit Eidgenössischem Berufsattest*) designed for youth who face difficulties at school, struggle to find a three or four-year apprenticeship, or risk dropping out. These programmes in Norway and Switzerland lead to qualifications that are recognised both on the labour market and within the education system, and allow graduates to continue into regular apprenticeship. Available evidence points to positive outcomes from these programmes. In Norway the programme is now being scaled up after a positive evaluation of the pilot. In Switzerland nearly half of the programme completers proceed to higher-level apprenticeships, and among those who do not, 75% find a job upon completion (Kis, 2016). The fact that these programmes end with a formal qualification is an important feature. (Kammermann et al., 2011) argues that two-year apprenticeships leading to a qualification are associated with better labour market outcomes than identical but uncertified programmes. In Switzerland in 2014, there were 5 900 students in two-year apprenticeship as compared to 61 000 in regular programmes (SERI, 2016).

Is a special apprenticeship an option for England?

Evidence from different countries, including Switzerland, suggests that special apprenticeship programmes designed for young people at risk can be effective. In the past many lower level apprenticeships (Level 2) were associated with lower quality and recent data confirm that in 2016/17 there were more people starting on higher-level apprenticeships while the uptake of Level 2 apprenticeships decreased (DfE, 2017). While an increase in higher-level apprenticeships can be seen as positive, it can leave aside some learners who are not be able to start immediately on a more demanding programme, as argued above. But an apprenticeship that leads to a lower level qualification can be a high-quality option, designed to provide strong support for the learner, with attention to a range of basic and transferable skills.

Policy issue 6.2: Supporting apprentices to successful completion

Challenge: Dropout

Apprentices with disadvantaged backgrounds are particularly at risk from dropout

Dropout from apprenticeship is a serious challenge in many countries. In England, two-thirds (67%) of starting apprentices complete (DfE SFA, 2017). In England, dropout can be less costly to the apprentice than in some other countries, because the apprenticeship is not tied to their employment. While methodological variations make it difficult to make precise comparisons of completion rates, completion rates are reported in the region of 50% for Australia, Canada, and New Zealand, above 60% for Ireland, over 70% in France but over 80% for Austria, Germany and Switzerland (OECD, 2014; Steedman, 2010 for Austria and France). Data from England show that apprentices from ethnic minorities, those with a learning difficulty or disability, and those with lower levels of education are all more likely to drop out (Gambin and Hogarth, 2016). In the Bern canton of Switzerland, around one-third of non-Swiss nationals drop out from apprenticeships, while among Swiss nationals, about one-fifth drop out. In Germany, dropout rates among foreign-born apprentices were up to 50% higher than among German-born apprentices (Autorengruppe Bildungsberichterstattung, 2016).

Alongside familiar causes of dropout, apprentices may drop out when they get another job

A US survey reports personal issues as the most common cause of dropout from apprenticeship, closely followed by performance problems on the job or in the classroom, and getting another job (Lerman et al., 2009). Employers attribute much dropout to a lack of effort on the part of the apprentice (Stalder and Schmid, 2006). In England, dropout has been associated with getting another job, moving to another educational programme and dropping out of education and training altogether. Academic and pastoral support for apprentices was widely agreed to be an important factor in ensuring completion, particularly for those apprentices aged 16 to 17 (Gambin, et al., 2014). Chapter 3 has argued that those who supervise apprentices in the workplace need more effective preparation to support younger apprentices, and help them through to completion.

More demanding apprenticeships in England could cause higher dropout rates

In England, the development of new more demanding apprenticeship standards and assessments implies, other things being equal, that dropout and failure rates will rise, either because apprentices feel they will be unsuccessful in the final assessment and therefore abandon the programme, or because they do in fact fail. Although there has been a lot of discussion of demanding standards and assessments, there has been much less discussion of the other side of this coin, of how apprentices can be helped to meet those higher demands. Training providers will do their best to minimise dropout, but may also want to concentrate their attention on learners and programmes where success is easy, rather than on those individuals facing very stretching programmes, who need a lot of support to complete successfully. But it is exactly these individuals who will benefit most from the programme in terms of enhanced skills, qualifications and life chances.

Policy pointer 6.2: Supporting apprentices to successful completion

Consider establishing an apprenticeship support service. Through that service, offer targeted support to assist through to completion apprentices in need, or at risk. Such measures may include additional training in basic skills, mentoring and coaching, and other work-based measures.

Analysis: What works in ensuring successful completion

Targeted help for apprentices in difficulty is available in some countries

In academic education, there is a relatively well understood set of approaches designed to support those who struggle in the classroom. In strong school systems, those facing the greatest challenges receive extra coaching, formally or informally; mentoring is offered; wider personal or social problems affecting school performance are addressed (see for example Field, Kuczera and Pont, 2007). In some countries, apprentices may receive similar support when they face difficulties, designed to help them complete. This is often the responsibility of local authorities. For example, in Germany 'apprenticeship assistance', available to apprentice dropouts, supports transition into another apprenticeship or training programme. Assistance includes remedial education (language skills, theoretical and practical instruction) and support with homework and exams (see Box 6.2 for some further examples).

Employers may be more willing to take on apprentices at risk if they know that support is available

From an employer's point of view, taking on an apprentice with learning challenges will be a risk. But they may be more willing to take this risk if they know they will receive support during the apprenticeship to ensure completion. So one of the potential benefits of targeted support to apprentices at risk is not only that it will help completion, but also that it may help young people facing challenges to obtain a good quality apprenticeship in the first place.

Some studies suggest that support offered to apprentices can improve the chances of completion

Although evidence is patchy, studies suggest that support should help promote successful completion. An Australian study of apprenticeship completion found that many apprentices felt a lack of support and did not know who to contact for assistance, leading them to drop out (Snell and Hart, 2008). The interim evaluation of the Australian Apprenticeships Mentoring Package (Deloitte Access Economics, 2014) found that a credible party, independent of the employer and apprentice, can help address issues that may lead to dropout, such as problems in personal life, health issues and problems in the workplace.

Box 6.2. Support services for apprentices at risk

In Australia, the Apprenticeship Support Network aims to help employers to recruit, train and retain apprentices and apprentices to succeed. 11 regional networks provide advice and support services for employers and apprentices through: universal services for all employers and apprentices, essential administrative support, payment processing and regular contact; targeted services for employers and apprentices needing additional support to complete the apprenticeship. New targeted in-training support services, such as mentoring, will, where there is a risk of non-completion, help apprentices and employers to work through issues and difficulties; and assistance to individuals who may be unsuited to an apprenticeship to identify alternative training pathways. Australia, like England, has a competitive training market with providers competing for students. By establishing the Network the government aimed to create efficiencies and reduce confusion in the market through a one-stop-shop for employers. Services provided by the Network are funded by the Australian Government and delivered by private providers. While it is too early to evaluate this initiative, stakeholders involved note that in the market of third parties (such as Australian Apprenticeship Support Network providers) there is potential for them to 'trip over each other' and be destructively competitive.

In Austria, integrative VET programmes (Integrative Berufsausbildung, IBA) target young people with special needs (two-thirds of participants), disabled youth and those without a school-leaving certificate. Training assistants, typically with experience with disadvantaged youth, provide specialist support to the young people involved. When IBA takes place at a training company, training assistants oversee administrative tasks, define the content of the training contract between the apprentice and the training company, prepare company employees for the arrival of the apprentice, and register the apprentice at the vocational school. Training assistants also act as mediators, provide tutorial support and design the final exam for the partial qualification pathway. When IBA takes place at a supra-company training centre, training assistance is provided by the centre's social workers.

In Germany, apprenticeship assistance (Ausbildungsbegleitende Hilfen) is available to young people taking an apprenticeship, as well as those who dropout, and supports the transition into another apprenticeship (or training programme). Assistance includes remedial education (language skills, theoretical and practical instruction) and support with homework and exams, which helps to overcome learning difficulties. Socio-pedagogical assistance (including mentoring) is also available, and this includes support with everyday problems and mediation with the training company, school trainers and family. The service is provided according to a support plan developed in partnership with the young person concerned. It is delivered through individual assistance at least three hours per week; there are also small group sessions. One particular aim is to reach out to youth with learning difficulties and those disengaged from school.

In Switzerland, young people enrolled in two-year apprenticeships can receive individual coaching (Fachkundige individuelle Begleitung) designed to help them improve their academic, technical and social skills. Swiss cantons are responsible for implementation under a national framework and guidelines. Around half of the two-year apprentices take up this offer, mostly to tackle weak language skills, learning difficulties or psychological problems. Most coaches are former teachers (of vocational or special needs education), learning and speech therapists or social workers. They receive targeted training, which may vary across cantons. For example, in Zürich they must attend a 300-hour course and participate in regular team-coaching sessions. Apprentices may also attend remedial lessons at vocational schools. For example, in Vaud canton, apprentices may take time off during their work placement to attend school for remedial classes.

Source: Kis, V. (2016), "Work-based learning for youth at risk: Getting employers on board", *OECD Education Working Papers*, No. 150, http://dx.doi.org/10.1787/5e122a91-en; and for Australia, Australian Apprenticeships (2017), "Australian Apprenticeship Support Network", www.australianapprenticeships.gov.au/australian-apprenticeship-support-network.

Dropout will be a key challenge of a reformed apprenticeship system in England

Dropout has received relatively little attention in the development of standards or in the operation of the levy. This is unfortunate, as if apprenticeship is to work as a vehicle for social mobility, young people, sometimes from highly disadvantaged backgrounds, are going to need a lot of support to assist them through to the successful completion of a demanding apprentice standard that will open the door to a successful career. Part of the answer to dropout lies in effective preparation of apprentices, and therefore in effective pre-apprenticeship and other forms of preparation, which provide relevant study skills to apprentices before they start their programmes, as discussed above. But, however well they are prepared, apprentices will face challenges during their training, and many will need active support of different types. The funding structure should encourage training providers to offer some support to apprentices. But training providers lack incentives to address several types of problem that may arise – for example when there are problems between the apprentice and the employer, or when the apprentice complains about poor quality training by the provider, or when the apprentice believes they should abandon their apprenticeship in favour of some other career or learning choice.

An independent apprenticeship support service, perhaps drawing on the Australian model, could be considered

England should consider establishing an independent apprenticeship support service to assist and support apprentices facing difficulties in completing their apprenticeship. While this is not designed to remove the responsibility from the training provider, and the employer, to do everything in their power to realise a successful completion, it recognises that apprentices may have needs that go beyond what employers and providers are in a position to offer, and beyond what they sometimes offer in practice. Such support might be provided at the request of the apprentice, but employers and training providers might also refer an apprentice in difficulty. An apprenticeship support service might also offer other services including services to employers, on the model of the Apprenticeship Support Network in Australia.

References

Autorengruppe Bildungsberichterstattung (2016), *Bildung in Deutschland*, www.destatis.de/DE/Publikationen/Thematisch/BildungForschungKultur/Bildungsstand/BildungDeutschland5210001169004.pdf?__blob=publicationFile.

Beck, V., A. Fuller and L. Unwin (2006a), "Increasing risk in the 'scary' world of work? Male and female resistance to crossing gender lines in apprenticeships in England and Wales", *Journal of Education and Work*, Vol.19/3, pp. 271-289.

Beck, V., A. Fuller and L. Unwin (2006b), "Safety in stereotypes? The impact of gender and 'race' on young people's perceptions of their post-compulsory education and labour market opportunities", *British Educational Research Journal*, Vol.32 /5, pp. 667-686.

BIS (2015), "Traineeships: First year process evaluation. Executive summary", *BIS Research Paper*, No. 222a, www.gov.uk/government/uploads/system/uploads/attachment_data/file/412623/BIS-15-195-traineeships-first-year-process-evaluation-executive-summary.pdf.

Bonin, H. et al. (2013), Evaluation zentraler ehe-und familienbezogener Leistungen in Deutschland, Prognostica.

DfE (Department for Education) (2017), *Further Education and Skills in England, October 2017*, www.gov.uk/government/uploads/system/uploads/attachment_data/file/650515/SFR53_2017_FINAL.pdf.

DfE SFA (2017), "National achievement rates tables 2015 to 2016", www.gov.uk/government/statistics/national-achievement-rates-tables-2015-to-2016.

Dolado, J. (2015), *How can Europe Reduce Youth Unemployment? World Economic Forum Report*, www.weforum.org/agenda/2015/02/can-europe-reduce-youth-unemployment/.

Field, S., M. Kuczera and B. Pont (2007), *No More Failures: Ten Steps to Equity in Education*, OECD Publishing, Paris, http://dx.doi.org/10.1787/9789264032606-en.

Fuller, A. and L. Unwin (2014), "The challenges facing young women in apprenticeships", in I. Schoon and J. Eccles (Eds.), *Gender Differences in Aspirations and Attainment*, Cambridge University Press, Cambridge.

Gambin, L., C. Hasluck and T. Hogarth (2014), *Maximizing Apprenticeship Completion Rates in England*, http://caf-fca.org/wp-content/uploads/2014/09/Maximizing-Apprenticeship-Completion-Rates-in-England.pdf.

House of Commons (2016), "Compendium of apprentice statistics", *Briefing Paper 06113*, http://researchbriefings.parliament.uk/ResearchBriefing/Summary/SN06113#fullreport.

Kammermann, M., B.E. Stalder and A. Hättich (2011), "Two-year apprenticeships - a successful model of training?", *Journal of Vocational Education & Training*, Vol. 63/3, pp. 377-396, http://dx.doi.org/10.1080%2F13636820.2011.586130.

Karmel T. and D. Oliver (2011), "Pre-apprenticeship and their impact on apprenticeship completion and satisfaction", *NCVER Occasional Paper*, http://files.eric.ed.gov/fulltext/ED517921.pdf.

Keep, E and S. James (2011), "Employer demand for apprenticeships", in T Dolphin and T Lanning (eds.) (2011), *Rethinking Apprenticeships*, IPPR, London.

Kis, V. (2016), "Work-based learning for youth at risk: Getting employers on board", *OECD Education Working Papers*, No. 150, OECD Publishing, Paris, http://dx.doi.org/10.1787/5e122a91-en.

Kuczera, M., S. Field and C. Windisch (2016), *Building Skills for All: A Review of England. Policy Insights from The Survey of Adult Skills*, www.oecd.org/edu/skills-beyond-school/building-skills-for-all-review-of-england.pdf.

Landert, C. and D. Eberli (2015), *Solutions Transitoires au Moment de la Transition I – États des Lieux*, On behalf of SBFI (State Secretariat for Education Research and Innovation), Landert Brägger Partner, Zurich, www.sbfi.admin.ch/berufsbildung/01501/01503/index.html?lang=fr.

Lerman, R. I., L. Eyster and K. Chambers (2009), *The Benefits and Challenges of Registered Apprenticeship: The Sponsors' Perspective*, The Urban Institute, https://wdr.doleta.gov/research/FullText_Documents/The%20Benefits%20and%20Challenges%20of%20Registered%20ApprenticeshipThe%20Sponsors%20Perspetive%20-%20Final%20Report.pdf.

Ministère de l'Éducation nationale, de l'Enseignement supérieur et de la Recherche (2017), EDUSCOL website, http://eduscol.education.fr/cid55994/pre-apprentissage.html.

Muehlemann, S. (2016), "The cost and benefits of work-based learning", *OECD Education Working Papers*, No. 143, OECD Publishing, Paris, http://dx.doi.org/10.1787/5jlpl4s6g0zv-en.

Norwegian Ministry of Education (n.d), *Certificate of Practice*, www.oecd.org/education/school/45158199.pdf.

OECD (2014), G20-OECD-EC Conference on Quality Apprenticeship, Country Information on Apprenticeships: Country Responses, www.oecd.org/els/emp/Youth%20questionnaire%20country%20responses-Compilation1.pdf.

Pullen, C. and J. Dromey (2016), *Earning and Learning: Making the Apprenticeship System Work for 16-18 Year Olds,* IPPR, www.ippr.org/files/publications/pdf/earning-and-learning_Nov2016.pdf?noredirect=1.

Quintini, G. and S. Martin (2006), "Starting well or losing their way? The position of youth in the labour market in OECD countries", *OECD Social, Employment And Migration Working Papers*, No. 39, http://dx.doi.org/10.1787/351848125721.

Social Mobility and Child Poverty Commission (2016), *Apprenticeships, Young People, and Social Mobility,* The Social Mobility and Child Poverty Commission's submission to the Apprenticeships Inquiry by the sub-committee on Education, Skills and the Economy, March 2016.

State Secretariat for Education and Innovation (SERI) Swiss Confederation (2016), *Vocational and Professional Education and Training in Switzerland*, SERI, www.eda.admin.ch/content/dam/countries/countries-content/canada/en/Vocational-and-professional-education-and-training-switzerland_E.pdf.

Steedman, H. (2010), *The State of Apprenticeship in 2010: International Comparisons*, http://cep.lse.ac.uk/pubs/download/special/cepsp22.pdf.

Chapter 7. Different sectors of apprenticeship in England

Apprenticeships in England are exceptionally diverse. This chapter looks at the issues arising in three special types of apprenticeship: those at degree level, those in smaller employers and those in the public sector. Degree apprenticeships are likely to grow rapidly as they allow those involved to avoid student loans and subsequent debt. This will be a positive development, but only if it restructures university degrees into quality apprenticeships, rather than just a part-time degree plus a job. Small employers play a big role in apprenticeship provision, and may need special support, including advice on how to make the most effective use of apprenticeship. The rationale for the new apprentice target for public-sector employers is questionable, given that the public-sector workforce is already relatively skilled in comparison with the private sector. Targets for the public sector might therefore be better limited to the use of youth apprenticeship as a recruitment tool.

Introduction: Focus on three sectors

This chapter looks at different sectors of apprenticeship

Apprenticeships in England are exceptionally diverse, and what works for some parts of the apprenticeship system may have little relevance in others. This chapter therefore looks at some of the issues arising in three subsectors. It examines apprenticeships at degree level, for smaller employers and in the public sector.

Policy issue 7.1: Securing a constructive use of degree apprenticeships

Challenge: Responding to rapid growth in degree apprenticeships with effective regulation

Levy arrangements will promote a rapid growth of degree apprenticeships

There has been growth, from a very low base, of higher (Level 4 and above) and 'degree' apprenticeships (Level 6 and 7). This has been actively encouraged as part of a broader objective of raising the 'level' of the apprenticeship system. This trend is now set to continue and accelerate, partly because of the policy emphasis, but more significantly because the new levy funding arrangements create powerful incentives to establish degree apprenticeships.

Degree apprenticeships involve university studies alongside full-time employment

Degree apprenticeships, developed in collaboration with universities, will take between one and six years, and like other apprenticeships must involve full-time (30 hours a week) employment alongside university studies. They are open to all ages, but are primarily targeted at 18-year-olds as an alternative to ordinary university study. Two models are possible: existing degree programmes can be combined with additional vocational training, with a separate test of professional competence at the programme's conclusion; alternatively, the employer and partner university co-design a fully-integrated course of study and on-the-job training (see Prospects, 2017). Some issues related to final assessment remain ambiguous, in particular how the end-point assessment associated with the apprenticeship standard relates to university exams leading to a degree award.

New levy funding arrangements create strong incentives to establish degree apprenticeships

For students on degree apprenticeships, all fees are paid, mostly from the levy pot, so that unlike most other university graduates, graduates of degree apprenticeships will end up free of tuition-related debt. From the employer point of view, it may be possible to train recruits for higher-level skills, taking advantage of the levy pot, potentially replacing expensive tailored training for recruits and/or costly graduate recruitment schemes. More than half of the larger employers surveyed by BPP University reported that they would be replacing graduate recruitment schemes with degree apprenticeships, and around one-third would do the same with sponsored degrees (BPP University, 2017). Some key employers, such as hospital trusts and other parts of the public sector, may also need to expand apprenticeships to meet the government's apprenticeship target, and could take advantage of degree apprenticeships to that end. For their part, universities are likely to see degree apprenticeships as a new 'income stream and business opportunity' (Universities UK, 2016). Given all these incentives, and encouragement from government, rapid growth in degree apprentices is a certainty.

Policy pointer 7.1: Securing a constructive use of degree apprenticeships

The expansion of degree apprenticeships should be a means of ensuring that the benefits of integrated on and off-the-job training are realised in these programmes rather than a means of restructuring full-time degrees as part-time merely to attract levy funds. To this end, ensure that all degree apprenticeships involve a clear commitment from employers to provide a substantial element of on-the-job training, closely aligned with the programme of studies pursued in a university. This proposal draws on the expectations for on-the-job training discussed in Chapter 3, and policy pointer 3.1.

Analysis: An opportunity to link growth to quality

Degree apprenticeships potentially offer the benefits of integrated learning and working

Degree apprentices will be working, and hopefully learning on the job, in relevant employment while they are studying. Potentially this has many advantages, as theoretical studies can be applied in practical contexts, while experience in practice can also inform theoretical learning; these classical benefits of apprenticeships can be realised at university degree level as well as other levels of education. Chapter 3 of this report argued for the importance of on-the-job learning in apprenticeship in general, drawing on the experience of other countries where this form of learning occupies a more central role in apprenticeship systems. Often, the apprenticeship model, with a blend of working and learning, is the right model to train for graduate level jobs.

Such an expansion should also benefit the entire apprenticeship 'brand'

Degree apprenticeships will also encourage people to see training for higher status professions through apprenticeship in a way that has been rare in the past. This is particularly important in the English context where many apprenticeships have involved low-level skills acquired quickly. Some of the status of university degrees should also come to be associated with degree apprenticeships and therefore with the apprenticeship brand. Degree apprenticeships should therefore be promoted *as apprenticeships*, in the face of evidence that some employers will be reluctant to describe degree and higher-level apprenticeships as such, because of the current low status of the apprenticeship brand (Gambin et. al., 2016; BPP University, 2017).

Degree apprenticeships are not a common model in other countries

Looked at across countries, the international equivalent of apprenticeships at above Level 3 are quite common internationally. For example, around one-quarter of those starting apprenticeships in Germany already have the Abitur (which grants the right to enter university), and this group have a disproportionate share of the highest status apprenticeships, often in big companies with very good career opportunities (Bliem et al., 2016). Degree apprenticeships are different, in that there are few international parallels of any scale. Perhaps the closest parallel is the 'dual university' programmes in Germany (see Box 7.1).

Box 7.1. Dual university programmes in Germany

Dual programmes combine a university course with employer-based practical training, employment or work experience. Students must also sign a contract with an employer. The curriculum is closely connected to a job, and the course is completed in two different places.

- Programmes with a training component combine a course of university study with training in a recognised occupation. In addition to the degree, students obtain a vocational qualification. Participants must normally have a general university entrance qualification and a contract of employment.
- Programmes with an employment component are primarily aimed at people who have already done vocational or professional training and/or have professional experience. It offers further professional development by combining a course of study with professional experience directly relevant to the course. Students may enrol without a general university entrance qualification. The amount of time the student spends in the classroom and at the place of work is agreed in a contract between the institution, the student and the employer.
- Programmes with a work experience component combine a course of study with extended practical phases with an employer. Students obtain a university degree but not a recognised vocational qualification. As a rule, this programme normally requires students to have a general university entrance qualification.

Source: Higher Education Compass, German Rectors' Conference (2017), "Dual programmes - Studying and work experience", www.hochschulkompass.de/en/degree-programmes/all-about-studying-in-germany/forms-of-study/dual-work-study-programmes.html.

Degree apprenticeships represent an opportunity

Degree apprenticeships represent a major opportunity, not only to extend the apprenticeship model into higher-level skills, but also to show-case apprenticeship that effectively integrates structured workplace experience and learning with off the job study in universities. Powerful incentives mean that employers and universities, *if* faced with the requirement for such integration, will respond positively – whereas in other sectors of apprenticeship employers might shy away from such requirements and avoid apprenticeship altogether. Such integration, show-cased in prestigious degree apprenticeships, might then provide a model for the whole apprenticeship sector.

But there are also risks

The new incentive structure will strongly encourage reorganisation of full-time university degree programmes with a large element of professional training (for example in teaching and nursing) into part-time programmes contributing to a degree apprenticeship. This could be positive if it reaps the full benefits of *integrated* work and learning, in which university studies are sequenced with particular forms of workplace experience in a co-ordinated way, maximising the value of the apprenticeship. Conversely, restructuring the university degree as a part-time programme, without any additional link with the working experience of students, would be no more than a device to attract levy funding for a university degree unchanged in substance save for being part-time. That would amount to a disruptive and wasteful distortion of the form of training provision just to meet the requirements of the levy. Looking at the literature and guidance currently available on degree apprenticeships, while the apprentice standards are documented in terms of the target knowledge, skills and behaviours required in the occupation, there is little or no evidence regarding how the workplace experience of those undertaking degree apprenticeships will be effectively integrated with university studies (e.g. see the detailed descriptions of existing degree apprenticeships linked to the UCAS website (UCAS, 2017). The funding rules for higher education institutions wishing to take part in degree apprenticeships unfortunately make no mention of any requirement on higher education institutions to integrate their programmes of study with workplace experience (see SFA, 2016).

Strong quality assurance is therefore necessary

Given this risk, strong quality requirements will be necessary to ensure that the degree apprenticeships offered genuinely add value as integrated programmes of work and study. This should reflect the principles and standards proposed for work-based learning in Chapter 3. The issue is not the quality of the university programme offered as part of the degree apprenticeship – which may already be quality assured in the form of degree programmes. Instead, quality assurance needs to apply to the working experience of degree apprentices, the extent to which that experience provides opportunities for effective learning, and the effective integration of that experience with university studies. This means quality assurance directed at the employer, as well as at universities. The underlying quality assurance issue, of ensuring integrated learning and working through an apprenticeship, rather than merely sticking some training on the side of employment, applies to all apprenticeships, not merely those at degree level. It is therefore encouraging to see that Ofsted is pushing for the authority to inspect employers taking part in degree apprenticeships (see FE Week, 2016). The OECD would support that approach, although given the importance of integrating university studies and work-based learning, a complete separation between the QAA (The Quality Assurance Agency for Higher Education) inspection regime in universities and Ofsted in the employers would not be desirable.

Quality in degree apprenticeships is vital if they are to replace employer-sponsored degrees

Employer-sponsored degrees involve an employer paying all or some university fees for their employee, and releasing their employee – often one day a week – to pursue the degree. 10% of students in UK universities – something over 200 000 students – are pursuing employer-sponsored degrees, including three-year degrees, but also HNC, HND, foundation and postgraduate degrees (Phoenix, 2017). This model is likely to be supplanted in large part by degree apprenticeships, since employers can call on levy funds to provide fees for such apprenticeships, but cannot do so for employer-sponsored degrees – one-third of large employers surveyed said that they expected to pursue this replacement strategy (BPP University, 2017). Employer-sponsored degrees have some potential advantages over degree apprenticeships – cost-sharing between employer and employee can be individually negotiated, as can release terms and the degree programme. Degree apprenticeships might be preferable if they fully reap the traditional advantages of apprenticeship – work-based learning closely integrated with university studies designed to realise the occupational competences as defined by employers. This underlines the importance of insisting that degree apprenticeships should have all of these qualities, and are not simply part-time degrees attached to a job – a model not preferable in substance to an employer-sponsored degree.

Policy issue 7.2: Supporting small and medium-sized employers (SMEs)

Challenge: Barriers and opportunities for apprenticeship among SMEs

It is often argued that apprenticeship may be less attractive to a smaller employer

Smaller employers may find it harder to retain skilled graduate apprentices, so the benefit of investing in their training is less than for larger employers (OECD, 2010; Johanson, 2009; Dar et al., 2003; CEDEFOP, 2008). There are also typically minimum administrative fixed costs associated with taking an apprentice, and these may also be an entry barrier for smaller employers. It is therefore widely asserted that smaller employers face particular barriers in making use of apprenticeship.

But in some countries at least, apprenticeship is more common in smaller firms

Surveys of employers offer evidence of whether employers participate or not in training, according to firm size. Such statistics are widely cited to show that training is more common in larger firms (see for example Stone and Braidford, 2008). But it should not be surprising that 'some' training is more likely in giant firms than in tiny ones. More telling statistics reveal the extent of training, taking into account the number of employees. Here the evidence is much less clear. In fact, smaller employers in some countries with large apprenticeship systems are sometimes *more* likely to take on apprentices, taking into account firm size. In Switzerland, the ratio of apprentices to total employees (the training ratio) was between 7.5% and 9% in companies with less than 10 employees, 4% in companies with 50-99 employees, and 3% in companies with 1 000+ employees. Similarly, in Austria, this same ratio was 5% in companies with less than 50 employees but just under 4% for companies with more than 50 employees. Germany displays a slightly different pattern, with a training ratio of 3% in companies with less than 10 employees, but 4% on average overall (Bliem et al., 2016).

In England, the training ratio is highest in midsize employers

Midsize employers (10 to 99 employees) had 11 apprentices per 1 000 employees); this was around twice the level found among both larger and smaller employers (DfE, 2016). It is striking that in England nearly half of all apprenticeship starts were in smaller employers, with less than 50 employees, and a further 15% of starts in medium-sized employers (between 50 and 250 employees).

The reasons for these patterns are unclear

So, while there are some clear theoretical explanations for why one might expect apprenticeship to be less common in small employers, the evidence on this is mixed, and in England it is midsize employers (10-99 employees) that appear to make most use of apprenticeship, taking account of their size. Sectoral factors could be relevant, for example, where small firms are more common in apprentice-rich fields. But it could also be that smaller employers, despite the barriers, find ways of taking advantage of apprenticeships. In some small firms, personal loyalties, combined with a large measure of firm-specific skills that take time to acquire – such as good relationships with customers – may mean that these employers may place a very high value on long-term employee retention, and skills development over time, resulting in a commitment to apprenticeship and rewarding the apprentice graduate. Conversely the apprentice graduate may find that their many useful firm-specific skills are not easily marketable to other employers. This is speculation but, whatever the precise factors at work, SMEs should be promising territory for the development of apprenticeships.

Policy pointer 7.2: Supporting small and medium-sized employers

Small employers already make extensive use of apprenticeship in England. To support further growth and enhance quality, facilitate support services for smaller employers, advising them on how to make most effective use of apprenticeship, and supporting local networks of co-operation between employers with apprentices.

Analysis: Facilitating apprenticeship in smaller employers

Smaller employers are an opportunity rather than an obstacle for apprenticeships

Countries where apprenticeship is common among smaller employers often pursue special support measures. For example in Germany there are different models: a lead enterprise may bear the overall responsibility for training, but parts of the training are conducted in various partner enterprises; alternatively some of the periods of training may take place outside the regular (small) enterprise, perhaps in a nearby large enterprise with a training workshop on the basis of reimbursement of training costs; several SMEs may work together and take on trainees; or the SMEs may establish an organisation which takes over the administrative tasks (contracts, etc.), while the individual enterprises offer the training (Poulsen and Eberhardt, 2016). Across countries, consultation services and arrangements to group SMEs together to make use of levies are also important (see Box 7.2) (See also Kuczera, 2017).

Apprentices in small companies may find external support particularly helpful

Smaller employers with less experience of apprenticeships may need external help during an apprenticeship. SMEs may need advice on how to use and manage apprentices, how to supervise them in the workplace, and how to work with other SMEs to pool experience and provide mutual support. This type of service may be critical not only to encouraging SMEs to take on apprentices, but also to providing apprenticeships of good quality that will lead to rewarding careers. A study in Australia found that in larger companies, mentoring services and buddy schemes were more common than in smaller firms. In small firms there is no dedicated human resources department where an apprentice may pursue a grievance (Dickie, McDonald and Pedic, 2011).

Box 7.2. Helping SMEs get the most out of training

In Spain, two non-governmental organisations (NGOs) (Fundación Bertelsmann and the JP Morgan Chase Foundation) collaborated to provide free technical support to SMEs interested in developing apprenticeship programmes. The pilot initiative focused on firms with between 10 and 500 employees. A consulting team worked with 190 SMEs to support them through the process of creating apprenticeship places, including identifying positions within the company which could be filled by apprentices and matching available VET qualifications with firm's skill needs. Of the 190 firms that the team worked with, 115 expect to offer at least one apprenticeship position during 2016/17 and 2017/18 – suggesting that technical support can help SMEs to overcome non-financial barriers in providing apprenticeships.

In Korea, the Korean SMEs Training Consortium Project was launched to help SMEs provide in-service training and retrain unemployed workers. A training consortium (TC) of SMEs forms an operating committee (OC) composed of representatives of TC members, local Chamber, Ministry of Labour field office, and training experts to manage its training tasks. The consortium established an information network among TC members, conducted training-needs surveys of each member SME; planned training activities and contracted outside training providers; collaborated to develop training programmes and materials; and conducted evaluations of major training courses. The objective was to provide a group of SMEs with training specialists, financed by public funds, to relieve the organisational, informational, and financial constraints that SMEs face in developing their human resources. The project promoted SME workers' productivity, solving the most critical SME problem of skilled manpower shortages, and provided preferential financial benefits to SMEs. The project also helped training policy to become more demand-driven by developing new working relationships between SMEs and training providers; and promoted partnership between private sector associations and public/non-governmental organisations.

Source: OECD (2017), *Getting Skills Right: Good Practice in Adapting to Changing Skill Needs: A Perspective on France, Italy, Spain, South Africa and the United Kingdom*; http://dx.doi.org/10.1787/9789264277892-en; Lee, K.W. (2016), *Skills Training by Small and Medium-Sized Enterprises: Innovative Cases and the Consortium Approach in the Republic of Korea*, Asian Development Bank Institute.

Policy issue 7.3: Underpinning the public-sector target with wider policy goals

Challenge: A new target for public-sector apprenticeships and its rationale

In England impetus is being given to public-sector apprenticeships through a new proposed target

The Labour Force Survey (BIS, 2016) shows that, in England, currently just 0.6% of public-sector employees are apprentices, meaning that the number of apprentices will need to be quadrupled for public-sector bodies to hit the 2.3% target (CIPFA, 2017). In some other countries, apprenticeship is only slightly less common in the public sector than it is in the private sector. In Germany, apprentices as a percentage of the workforce are 3% in the public sector and 4% in private industry; in Switzerland, the comparable figure was 5% in the public sector, not far off the private sector average (Bliem et al., 2016). The target will work in tandem with the incentives created by the levy. Among a group of public-sector employers surveyed on their likely response to the levy and the public-sector target, half said that they would reduce graduate recruitment, and three-fifths said that they would reduce sponsored degrees in favour of apprenticeships. They are likely to expand higher-level apprenticeships, in particular. None of the employers surveyed planned to pay apprentices the minimum wage (BPP University, 2017).

Policy pointer 7.3: Underpinning the public-sector target with wider policy goals

The public-sector workforce has better skills, on average, than the private sector. Any targets for the public sector might therefore be limited to the use of apprenticeship as a recruitment tool, in particular for youth apprenticeship.

Analysis: Different rationales for recruitment and for upskilling the existing workforce

The government sets out two rationales for the new target

The government's consultation paper argues for the target in relation to two goals: first, in transitioning young people into the labour market; second in upskilling the existing workforce. Government itself, it can be argued, needs to demonstrate its own commitment to such objectives if it is to credibly persuade private sector employers to share them (BIS, 2016).

Governments normally take more responsibility for the transition from school to work, than for upskilling the workforce

As discussed in Chapter 2, the transitioning of young people between school and work is a policy domain in which government in England, as in most OECD countries, has taken a full and active responsibility, in higher and further education as well as in apprenticeship and other forms of vocational training. Substantial flows of government money go into supporting this process, [including higher education given the RAB (The Resource Accounting and Budgeting) charge despite the increased fees in recent years]. Apprenticeship for school leavers can reasonably expect to be part of this process, and Chapter 2, argued that special attention should therefore be paid to the promotion of youth apprenticeship. Conversely, upskilling the workforce, while important and desirable, is not a field where government has been so directly involved, and where funding levels have usually been more modest.

Some other countries are also seeking to develop apprenticeships in the public sector

Norway is currently, like England, seeking to expand apprenticeships in the public sector through a range of initiatives and targets. But apprenticeship in Norway is overwhelmingly an institution serving the needs of young people in upper secondary education (alongside employers), and transitioning them into employment (see Box 7.3). This means that the rationale for the public-sector targets in Norway is quite different to that in England.

Public-sector workers already have better skills than average, so further upskilling does not appear as a priority

In England, public-sector workers have better skills than private sector workers on average, and that skills gap appears to be widening, partly because of outsourcing of low-skilled jobs from the public to the private sector. As pointed out by Amin-Smith et al., (2017), nearly two-thirds of public-sector workers had completed post-secondary education in 2015-16, compared with only 38% in the private sector. At the same time, indications from public-sector employers surveyed suggest that quite a lot of emphasis will be given to higher-level apprenticeships (BPP University, 2017). While upskilling the existing public-sector workforce might still be desirable, it should not be a policy priority, and it does not appear to be an equity priority, given the concentration of low skills in the private sector.

There are other more flexible ways of encouraging the use of apprenticeships in the public sector.

Exempting the upskilling of incumbent workers in the public sector from the target would not mean ignoring the potential of apprenticeships in this domain. Other measures are possible to raise the profile of apprenticeships in the public sector, but such measures could be local and flexible, and respond to business needs (see Box 7.4). Other recent studies, including the report of the select committee, and the Institute for Fiscal Studies (IFS), have also argued against a blanket target for the public sector (House of Commons, 2017; Amin-Smith et al., 2017).

Box 7.3. Apprenticeships in the public sector in Norway

Norway has launched an initiative designed to increase the number of apprentices employed by central government. The new strategy makes it mandatory for all government agencies to have at least one apprentice. This is part of a broader strategy to increase the number of apprentices by 20%, linked to an increase in the employer subsidy for taking apprentices. The strategy includes measures to make it easier to provide apprentices with high-quality training, to spread information about the advantages of having apprentices, the need for competence-building, and measures for recruiting instructors.

The Norwegian government is also introducing a requirement for companies to have an apprenticeship programme to be eligible for major public procurements. Universities and university colleges have been asked to increase their apprenticeships by 50%.

Source: Government.no (2017), "More apprenticeships", www.regjeringen.no/en/topics/education/school/innsiktsartikler/the-vocational-education-and-training-vet-promotion/more-apprenticeships/id2466569.

Box 7.4. Public-sector contribution in the London Apprenticeship Campaign

The public sector was expected to play a significant role in the London Apprenticeship Campaign in driving up the number of apprentices, encouraging private sector employers to do the same. London Councils saw joining the campaign as an invaluable opportunity to bring more young people into an aging workforce, integrate those not in education or employment, and influence local businesses to do the same. It launched the London Councils apprenticeship project in 2009 and established a sub-group to support delivery of the target of taking on over 2 000 new apprentices in the city by 2012 within London Councils and partner organisations. The sub-group included representatives of boroughs, NAS, UNISON (a key public-sector trade union), a Further Education representative and Sector Skills Councils. The body devised a London Borough Apprenticeship Plan which identified several key activities to be carried out, including sharing best practice, networking events, lobbying Sector Skills Councils and others to work towards apprenticeship frameworks, and putting in place more pathways to employment for skills shortage areas (London Councils, 2012). By March 2012 the boroughs had over-reached their target, delivering 2 714 apprenticeships in roles as diverse as animal attendants, social care and information and communication technology (ICT), with many progressing to advanced apprenticeships and permanent jobs.

Source: Evans, S. and G. Bosch (2012), "Apprenticeships in London: Boosting skills in a city economy - with comment on lessons from Germany", *OECD Local Economic and Employment Development (LEED) Working Papers*, No. 2012/08, http://dx.doi.org/10.1787/5k9b9mjcxp35-en.

References

Amin-Smith, N., J. Cribb and L. Sibieta (2017), *Reforms to Apprenticeship Funding in England,* Institute for Fiscal Studies, www.ifs.org.uk/uploads/publications/budgets/gb2017/gb2017ch8.pdf.

Bliem, W., A. Petanovitsch and K. Schmid (2016), *Dual Vocational Education and Training in Austria, Germany, Liechtenstein and Switzerland.* Institut für Bildungsforschung der Wirtschaft www.dcdualvet.org/wp-content/uploads/Dual-VET-Comparative-Study_Full-Study.pdf.

BIS (Department of Business, Innovation and Skills) (2014a), "Apprenticeships evaluation: Employers", *BIS Research Paper,* No. 204, www.gov.uk/government/uploads/system/uploads/attachment_data/file/387595/bis-14-1207-Apprenticeships-Evaluation-Employers-December-2014.pdf.

BIS (2014b), "Apprenticeships evaluation: Learners", *BIS Research Paper,* No. 205, www.gov.uk/government/uploads/system/uploads/attachment_data/file/387662/bis-14-1208-Apprenticeships-Evaluation-Learners-December-2014.pdf.

BIS (2016), *Consultation on Apprenticeship Targets for Public Sector Bodies,* www.gov.uk/government/uploads/system/uploads/attachment_data/file/494493/bis-16-24-apprenticeship-targets-for-public-sector-bodies.pdf.

BPP University (2017a), *Employer Guide: Apprenticeship Levy Study.* https://s3-eu-west-1.amazonaws.com/bppassets/public/assets/pdf/handbooks/bpp-guide-the-apprenticeship-levy-study.pdf.

BPP University (2017b), *The Apprenticeship Levy Study: Public Sector,* http://employers.bpp.com/assets/Public_Sector_Research.pdf.

CEDEFOP (2008), "Sectoral training funds in Europe", *European Centre for the Development of Vocational Training Panorama Series,* No. 156, Luxembourg.

CIPFA (2017), *The Levy, Apprenticeships and the Public Sector.*

Cribb, J., R. Disney and L. Sibieta (2014), *The Public Sector Workforce: Past, Present and Future IFS Briefing Note BN145,* Institute of Fiscal Studies, www.ifs.org.uk/bns/bn145.pdf.

Dar, A. and T. Whitehead (2003), *Training Levies: Evidence from Evaluations,* The World Bank, http://documents.worldbank.org/curated/en/2003/12/8913510/training-levies-evidence-evaluations.

Dickie, McDonald and Pedic, (2011), *A Fair Deal – Apprentices and their employers in NSW, Integrated Research Report,* BVET, Sydney.

DfE (Department for Education) (2016), *Apprenticeships Evaluation 2015 – Employers,* A report by IFF Research, with the Institute for Employment Research at the University of Warwick, www.gov.uk/government/uploads/system/uploads/attachment_data/file/562486/Apprenticeships_evaluation_2015_-_employers.pdf.

Evans, S. and G. Bosch (2012), "Apprenticeships in London: Boosting skills in a city economy - with comment on lessons from Germany", *OECD Local Economic and Employment Development (LEED) Working Papers,* No. 2012/08, OECD Publishing, Paris, http://dx.doi.org/10.1787/5k9b9mjcxp35-en.

FE Week (2016), "Exclusive: Ofsted wants key degree apprenticeship inspection role", FE Week, http://feweek.co.uk/2016/12/06/exclusive-ofsted-wants-key-degree-apprenticeship-inspection-role/.

Gambin, L. et al. (2016), *The Apprenticeship Levy: How Will Employers Respond? Department for Education Research Report,* www.gov.uk/government/uploads/system/uploads/attachment_data/file/562445/The_apprenticeship_levy_how_will_employers_respond.pdf.

Government.no (2017), "More apprenticeships", www.regjeringen.no/en/topics/education/school/innsiktsartikler/the-vocational-education-and-training-vet-promotion/more-apprenticeships/id2466569.

Higher Education Compass, German Rectors' Conference (2017), "Dual programmes - Studying and work experience", www.hochschulkompass.de/en/degree-programmes/all-about-studying-in-germany/forms-of-study/dual-work-study-programmes.html.

House of Commons, (2016), *House of Commons Briefing Paper Number 06152, 23 November 2016 Business Statistics.*

House of Commons (2017), *Apprenticeships. Second Joint Report of the Business, Energy and Industrial Strategy and Education Committees of Session 2016-17*, www.publications.parliament.uk/pa/cm201617/cmselect/cmese/206/206.pdf.

Institute for Fiscal Studies (2017), *IFS Green Budget 2017: Reforms to Apprenticeship Funding in England*, IFS, www.ifs.org.uk/publications/8863.

Johanson, R. (2009), "A review of national training funds", *SP Discussion Paper*, No. 0922, The World Bank, Washington, DC.

Kuczera, M. (2017), "Incentives for apprenticeship", *OECD Education Working Papers*, No. 152, OECD Publishing, Paris, http://dx.doi.org/10.1787/55bb556d-en.

Lee, K.W. (2016), *Skills Training by Small and Medium-Sized Enterprises: Innovative Cases and the Consortium Approach in the Republic of Korea*, Asian Development Bank Institute.

OECD (2017), *Getting Skills Right: Good Practice in Adapting to Changing Skill Needs: A Perspective on France, Italy, Spain, South Africa and the United Kingdom*; http://dx.doi.org/10.1787/9789264277892-en.

OECD (2013), *Skills Development and Training in SMEs*, OECD Publishing, Paris, http://dx.doi.org/10.1787/9789264169425-en.

OECD (2010), *Learning for Jobs*, OECD Publishing, Paris, http://dx.doi.org/10.1787/9789264087460-en.

Phoenix, D. (2017), *Making a Success of Employer-Sponsored Education, HEPI Report 83*, www.hepi.ac.uk/wp-content/uploads/2016/04/Making-a-success-of-Employer-Sponsored-Education-Report-83.pdf.

Poulsen S. and C. Eberhardt (2016), *Approaching Apprenticeship Systems from a European Perspective*, BIBB, Bonn.

Prospects (2017), Prospects website, www.prospects.ac.uk/jobs-and-work-experience/apprenticeships/degree-apprenticeships.

SFA (2016), *Apprenticeship Funding Rules for Higher Education Institutions 2016 to 2017, Version 1, March 2016*, www.gov.uk/government/uploads/system/uploads/attachment_data/file/604968/HEI_funding_rules.pdf.

Stone, I. and P. Braidford (2008), *Engaging Small Employers In Continuing Training: An International Review of Policies and Initiatives*, http://webarchive.nationalarchives.gov.uk/+/http:/www.ukces.org.uk/pdf/Report_30.pdf.

UCAS (2017), "Degree apprenticeships", www.ucas.com/ucas/undergraduate/getting-started/apprenticeships-uk/degree-apprenticeships.

Universities UK (2016), *The Future Growth of Degree Apprenticeships*, www.universitiesuk.ac.uk/policy-and-analysis/reports/downloads/FutureGrowthDegreeApprenticeships.pdf.

ORGANISATION FOR ECONOMIC CO-OPERATION AND DEVELOPMENT

The OECD is a unique forum where governments work together to address the economic, social and environmental challenges of globalisation. The OECD is also at the forefront of efforts to understand and to help governments respond to new developments and concerns, such as corporate governance, the information economy and the challenges of an ageing population. The Organisation provides a setting where governments can compare policy experiences, seek answers to common problems, identify good practice and work to co-ordinate domestic and international policies.

The OECD member countries are: Australia, Austria, Belgium, Canada, Chile, the Czech Republic, Denmark, Estonia, Finland, France, Germany, Greece, Hungary, Iceland, Ireland, Israel, Italy, Japan, Korea, Latvia, Luxembourg, Mexico, the Netherlands, New Zealand, Norway, Poland, Portugal, the Slovak Republic, Slovenia, Spain, Sweden, Switzerland, Turkey, the United Kingdom and the United States. The European Union takes part in the work of the OECD.

OECD Publishing disseminates widely the results of the Organisation's statistics gathering and research on economic, social and environmental issues, as well as the conventions, guidelines and standards agreed by its members.

OECD PUBLISHING, 2, rue André-Pascal, 75775 PARIS CEDEX 16
(91 2018 04 1 P) ISBN 978-92-64-29847-7 – 2018

www.ingramcontent.com/pod-product-compliance
Ingram Content Group UK Ltd.
Pitfield, Milton Keynes, MK11 3LW, UK
UKHW051506290926
15471UKWH00008B/1462

9 789264 298477